What is *Love?*

Story Republic Press
hello@storyrepublic.com

Ordering Information:
Quantity sales. Special discounts are available on quantity purchases by corporations, associations, and others. For details, contact the "Special Sales Department" at the address above.

What is Love? / Edited by Rumi Tsuchihashi —1st ed.
ISBN 9798330474479

Designer: Enrika Greathouse
Illustrator: Everette Fournier (pages 17 and 19)
Illustrator: Susan E (pages 56 and 130)
Uncredited photographs (pages 91,93,95)
Photographer: Adita Romansa (page 115)

What is Love?

A STORY COLLECTION

Edited by Rumi Tsuchihashi

Story Republic Press

For everyone who shares real-life stories with honesty and courage. May love beyond your conception take seed and blossom inside you.

Contents

Introduction

Can you define love? I tried, and it was hard.

Love is an emotion and a verb. It's as elusive as the holy grail but omnipresent. Love crosses realms, transcending time and even death. We look for it between lovers, teammates, children and parents and grandparents, healers and the ailing, teachers and students, humans and pets and the natural world. And we find it there. But, crushingly, not always.

Having edited this book, the one thing I know for sure about love is we make sense of it through our stories.

Take this example.

> It's July at the beach, two hours west of Tokyo. A young mother wearing a wide-brimmed straw hat arrives, carrying an enormous mesh bag in one arm and a baby in the other; the rest of the family is a step behind her.

She chooses a suitable spot and sets the ten-month-old down to spread a blanket. Immediately, things go wrong.

The baby girl takes off. Like a newly hatched sea turtle, she crawls toward the ocean wobbly but with all her might.

Mom fetches the baby. Baby takes off. After several rounds of this and no progress on laying the blanket, Mom's fuse gets short. The father steps in with a solution: He'll take the baby to the water's edge and hold her up by the armpits. The idea is a hit; the baby giggles, squeals, and splashes her toes.

The father returns to the spot triumphantly. But his daughter isn't done playing in the waves. She crawls away from the blanket at ten times the original speed. Now, Dad's got flared nostrils. The mood is tense.

Ojii-chan, the grandfather, lifts a hand to say, "Allow me."

He walks behind the fast-crawling baby but doesn't pick her up.

Not even when she reaches the shore. Or when the first wave splashes her face. He lets her continue for a second or two longer.

When he does lift the baby out of the water,

he doesn't walk her back to the blanket. He
takes five steps back and lets the little girl
crawl in again.

And again.
And again.
And again.
And again.
And again.

For decades, I thought this cringey formative story I
heard on repeat was about what a pain in the ass I was
from day one. But then, I reexamined it through the
lens of "What is love?" and everything changed.

Suddenly, I experienced the story through the eyes of
Ojii-chan, a man lit up by a grandchild's love of the
ocean at first sight. I felt his palpable delight in the
tedium of creating guardrails for a curious spirit.

"If this isn't love, I don't know what is," I thought
with wet eyes, my body limp with relief and gratitude.

Every single contributor to this book turned their life
stories over like a multi-faceted sphere, looking for
clues about what love is even when it hurt to do so.

The submissions hail from Canada, the U.S.,
Australia, New Zealand, the UK, Spain, and France;
several authors live thousands of miles away from

Germany, Ireland, India, and Japan, where they were
born or lived for part of their lives.

You're about to discover layered tales of wonder,
doubt, bewilderment, awe, disappointment, laughter,
and bliss that unfold in kitchens, cars, hospitals,
conference rooms, rural homes, boardwalks, and city
streets. Their narrative arcs go far beyond the tropes
of getting or losing the object of their affection.

If you suspect that love is far more expansive than
"love stories" suggest, this book is for you.

If you learn best about anything from lived examples,
and love is no exception, this book is for you.

If love confuses you, but you know it when you feel it
at the core of your being, this book is for you.

If you're intrigued by how we make sense of life and
love through the stories we tell ourselves—and each
other—this book is for you.

And if all you want is to sink into delicious writing,
slow your breath, and feel your heart open, then here
you go, and you're welcome.

Rumi Tsuchihashi

Executive Editor
Story Republic Press

"Nothing is mysterious, no human relation. Except love."

-Susan Sontag

PART 1

Love is:

tenderness.

Should I Tell Her?

For the last number of years, I have been making smoothies every morning for Shera and myself, which feels good to do.

It's a small moment we can share at the start of the day, and a routine investment in the bank of good husbandry.

Smoothie'ing is an art.

A nutritional canvas, painted upon the walls of two plastic personal size Ninja blender chalices, with only the finest frozen fruits available from aisle 4 of the 24-hour Super-Valu grocer down the street.

To fan the flame of surprise, and to uphold maximum mystery in our relationship, every day is a new recipe, and I take great pride in my work.

The results are always positive, which has fuelled a level of belief in my abilities as a suitable mate. I mean, what's not to like about waking up to a smoothie, creatively crafted by the love of your life?

I'm sitting across the table from my wife. She just launched into her morning routine of telling me about her crazy vivid dreams, and while doing so, takes a brief pause to have a sip.

As she speaks, something looks off.

Almost like part of her front tooth is missing.

Now I notice I've made a fatal mistake.

Blueberries.

A LOT of blueberries.

I put too many blueberries in our smoothies today. It appears that every single piece of every single one of them has staked a claim on all available white space in her mouth.

Now, I'm in an awful position.

Should I tell her?

At this point in my life, conflict, of any kind, is absolutely terrifying. I tend to freeze, stare blankly at my opposer for great lengths of time, and secretly wish for the colour and texture changing abilities of an octopus so I can disappear into my surroundings.

The sweat forming under my shirt is signaling an impending conflict is nigh, and I feel the freeze taking hold.

It's spreading faster with the thoughts:

"She only just woke up, and if I tell her, I'll make her feel embarrassed and awkward."

"If I tell her, I'll feel awkward and responsible for her embarrassment, because I'M THE ONE WHO MADE THE DAMN SMOOTHIE!!"

As it all rises internally, she mentions she's about to leave to visit someone, and has a particular look in her eye as she says it.

It's the look of pure joy that comes with reconnecting with a close friend, and she's excited because she hasn't seen this friend in a long time.

And here it is. The moment of truth.

Should I tell her?

Should I ruin her joy?

She seems so happy.

Before I have time for more thoughts, she stands up, heads towards the door, and for a brief second, I hear a voice inside my head say:

"Do it now, or suffer the consequences."

I acknowledge the voice, but the freeze has taken over.

I sit there, guitar on lap, my own smoothie in hand, helplessly watching her walk out of sight towards the bathroom.

I don't tell her.

Not more than a millisecond goes by, and I hear her tone, pitch, and volume of voice dramatically transform.

I'm afraid.

"MICHAEL!!!!! WHY DIDN'T YOU TELL ME I HAVE BLUEBERRIES IN MY TEETH!??!?!?!"

All that joy.

All that enthusiasm.

All that love, instantly flushed down the toilet because the bathroom mirror had more courage to convey what I could not.

My lack of response makes her furious, and she leaves abruptly. I'm left with the weight of it all settling on my shoulders, and into my heart. I feel buckets of guilt, shame, and every awful emotion that makes one regret their actions.

As I'm sitting there at our kitchen table in the aftershock of my poor husbandry, I begin plucking away at my guitar, and think about what love really is.

Love is so many things.

But the kind of love built between two people that results in happiness, instead of murder, depends on a few essential foundations. Today, I am reminded of the significance of honesty.

It all falls apart without honesty.

In the spirit of honesty, and to repent for my erroneous ways, I remain at the table to work through my feelings the best way I know how.

With my guitar.

About 90 minutes later, I finish the last line of a short song, just as I hear the front door open.

She speaks no words and avoids eye contact as she comes into the living room. Perhaps I got my octopus wish.

I fear she is still mad at me, but it's up to me now. Time to rally the courage, prove my worth as a mate, and overcome my freeze.

With all my might, I say "Shera, I have something to say to you."

She acknowledges my statement and sits down with open ears.

With that, I offer my apology with a song[1].

---

[1] To listen to the song, visit
https://michaelaverill.bandcamp.com/track/just-tell-her

Just tell her
You've been thinking it all morning
Just tell her
You owe her a proper warning
If you care at all about her needs
If you care about the air she breathes
If you care about her hopes and dreams
Just tell her
She has blueberries in her teeth

Michael Averill is a speaker, songwriter, and founder of the Write Songs You Love podcast. As a touring artist with a 20-year career, he's taken his music and stories to four continents, including a 4000-mile walk across Canada. In 2022, The Visioneers International Network recognized his efforts to foster environments that enhance the quality of life for humanity with a Lifetime Achievement Award for Music and Community Well-Being. Michael holds a bachelor's degree in health and wellness and lives in Kelowna, Canada, where he enjoys questioning words, creating goofy phrases, and walking his cat child, Pippin.

Love is Like Peanut Brittle

My mother tells me she knew after her first date she was going to marry my father.

True, the cobalt blue of his shiny new '57 Chevy, which matched his eyes, may have been what first turned her head.

But what she remembers more vividly was his kindness and charm. "We fell into a relationship like we'd been friends our whole lives," she recalls.

"I think I'm falling in love with you," he'd said early on. She didn't have to think about it. She already knew.

When he knew for sure, he proposed with the only engagement ring in the store that would fit her tiny finger.

While he behaved with much bravado and made most of the decisions in those early days, on the morning of their wedding he called her over and over just to check, asking, "You're going to show up, right?"

She did show up, always showed up, and is still showing up sixty-five years later.

Thinking back on their long marriage, it strikes me that their love is like peanut brittle.

Irresistible ambrosia becoming a sticky mess that melts into lingering sweetness.

It hasn't always been happily ever after.

When my dad was seventeen, his father died. Five years later, married to my mom with a new baby—my brother—he was scraping out a living at the paper mill when his mother died too.

We lived in a mill town. A drinking town. He fit right in.

Much later, when I got up the courage, I asked him about that. Why he drank so much.

"I was mad," he said. "After my mother's death, so soon after my dad's, I was just so goddamn mad."

The anger was a smoldering fuse ignited often with alcohol.

I spent many evenings of my youth riding my bike around town, tears streaming down my face, after witnessing the dad I idolized slip away into a bottle.

Yet, for the most part, he held his demons at bay, working hard to become a mill boss.

"Pretty rare for a dumb guy like me," he would say.

He was a good provider. A loving, caring father when he wasn't drinking. I wanted for nothing.

Well, except for a sober dad.

Like his father, he was a town leader involved in everything important to our small community—the hockey rink, the golf course, the fire department, even the church choir.

He turned his failed pro hockey career into being a popular coach, teaching hundreds of kids how to skate.

And the drinking? That was like his father too, except it didn't kill him.

The respect he earned for all his contributions died pretty fast when he hit the bottle. People can be quick to judge when they don't have all the facts.

When he'd sober up, he'd work at making things right with my mom.

He never, ever apologized to me. It wasn't hard for him to go back to being the dad I'd always adored. He really didn't have to work at that. Didn't seem to think he needed my forgiveness.

But I have forgiven him.

When I was sixteen, he quit drinking. Then he quit drinking again. Then, long after we thought he'd finally quit drinking—he quit for good.

He is now sober. But my beloved dad is disappearing again.

He is now sober. But a dimming of his mind is dulling his humour, blunting his laugh.

He is now sober. But staggering steps and slurring words feel eerily familiar.

My mother patiently answers the same questions over and over, hour after hour, day after day.

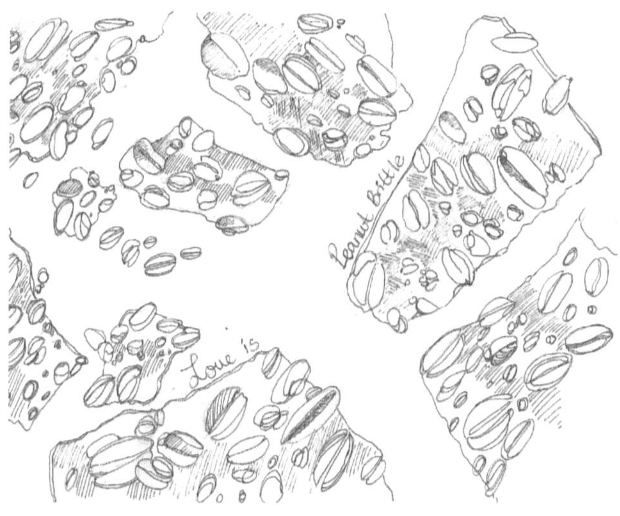

"Where are my shoes, my glasses, my paper, my lunch?" he asks. But never, thankfully, "Where are my memories of you?"

He still always remembers her, and she is still always there for him, which is what I recall from my childhood: my father struggling to do the right thing while fighting his demons; my mother offering her own steady resistance against those demons.

She was never a pushover. She served my father, like she did all of us, with love and strength.

My mother is as fierce as she is gentle when it comes to family—A mama bear who protected all of us when things got tough during my dad's drinking days and now, in his dementia.

With her wit, grit, and grace, she has always been the gale force wind that carries our family along. At eighty-five, she still is.

The gusts of her unconditional love are carrying me to the day when the weight of her responsibilities at the helm of our family falls to me. I hope I'll be ready when that day comes.
I look into her eyes. I've seldom seen them bitter or resentful. Rarely seen shadows of regret.

I ask her about her sixty-plus years with my dad.

What she recalls are those charming words, that first inkling of love, the honeyed kindness that drew her to him almost six and a half decades ago.

Loving him hasn't been easy and she is showing me, showing all of us, that retelling bitter stories isn't helpful.

The truth is known, forgiven, and wrapped in that sweetness she has chosen to remember instead.

There isn't much time.

Just enough to sort through the last broken pieces and savour the sweet, salty, sticky mess...that is love.

Leanne Fournier writes fiction, nonfiction, and poetry in the stunning wilderness of Northwestern Ontario, Canada. Her creative work is infused with vivid imagery and a profound sense of place, evident in her beautifully illustrated poetry collection. The collection explores the contradictions and parallels she sees around human connection and belonging—and is set to be released in 2025. Leanne founded MightyWrite—Write for Business, where she helps clients tell stories with clarity and impact and find their unique voice. A passionate writer and social justice advocate, Leanne publishes stories about the people most often unseen and unheard at mightywrite.substack.com.

Love in Hard Places

Against the dark sky
A million stars give evidence
Within dark rooms
A small light shines reverence
When shadows loom
light blooms
into a soft steady shimmer
Like the glimmer of gold
A sliver of hope
Whispers through darkness
A small ray of moonlight
Pierces through the midnight
illuminating the hard times
with Brilliance and Resilience
it is there she finds
LOVE

Of Heart, Hope, and Hurts

When I was nine, my dad was my hero. Fun, bright, and whimsical. He was the light I could count on until I couldn't.

Every Fourth of July, my dad would set up a flurry of fireworks that started on the porch and ended up in splendor late into the night in the middle of the street. He was the conductor of joy. Every afternoon, he would take me to the park and let me play until I either conked out or until sunset, whichever came first.

On Halloween when we'd go trick-or-treating my mom would only allow one candy per day from our stash, while my dad would sneak me a handful when she wasn't looking.

Every summer, on the first day of the county fair, he would make us take a nap in the middle of the day so we could last until midnight when the fair closed. This was our big day out. We did it every year without fail. Then, one year, we didn't go. That was the year he went away.

I remember the news floating around me like dandelions in the wind, The adults whispered and shook their heads in pity. My dad was in jail, and I didn't get to see him much anymore. I heard he got in a fight. Some people even said that he was on drugs.

But I didn't believe them. They didn't know him like I knew him.

I remember going to Papoo's house one weekend and noticing something had changed. Papoo was my dad's dad and I loved going over there because they had a big backyard, and we could get ice cream from the Ice Cream Man anytime we wanted. Something my grandmother, Sonia, my mom's mom (who I lived with), never let us do. But this time, when we got there, the first thing I did was look for my dad, but he wasn't there. The house felt cold and weird. I missed his playful laugh, and his trying to jump scare me from the different corners of the house.

Were the rumors true? I wondered where he was. Then I started to wonder how he was. I couldn't stop thinking about him. That night, I soaked my pillow with tears. Even if everyone else scoffed and whispered with judgment I still loved him and knew he loved me.

You can't see me like this.

A few weeks later, I was at my Papoo's house again.

And this time, my dad was home. I was so happy he was back. And things were back to normal. I was free as a bird. My dad was hanging with some friends in the back. I was playing World Wrestling Federation (WWF) wrestling with my brothers in the front yard. Then while I was right in the middle of a body slam. I faintly heard the melody of the Ice Cream Man coming. It was still a ways away, but I knew I had to act quickly.

I went through the open garage into the backyard to get some change from my dad. But he wasn't there. Hmmm, I thought, he was just here. I guess he and his friends went into the house. I opened the sliding glass door, to see if he was in the kitchen or living room. Nope, the house was empty.

Shoot, where did he go?

Finally, I quickly walked down the long hallway that ended at my dad's bedroom door. I could hear people inside... but the door was closed.

I turn the knob to go in, but it's locked. Hmmm, that's strange. It's never locked.

It's been a few minutes, and I can hear the Ice Cream Man's chime getting louder. He's almost here.

"Daddy," I call out his name and knock on the door with immediacy and confidence. I know he's in there, but he's not responding. I knock louder.

"Daddy! Open the door." I hear nothing, just silence.

The Ice Cream Man's chime sang even louder now. He's on our street.

I put my ear to the door and hear musings of conversations and movement. I won't give in. I start to bang on the door with more conviction.

"Daaaaddy!!" I yelp in frustration. The door finally cracks open. My dad peeks his head out. His eyes big, bulging, and bloodshot. He wipes away tears and whispers

"I don't want you to see me like this." Then with a soft sadness, he shuts the door.

I am left standing there, staring at the grain of the cedar wood door. My eyes are fixed on the bright brass doorknob.

In the background, I hear the Ice Cream Man's chime fading away until I no longer hear its song.

I feel numb.

It is in this moment that I first learn the rumors are true. My dad is on drugs and he is getting high right behind this door. I'm heartbroken but somehow without pain that stings. Instead, I feel a certain dull awareness and keen sadness.

Even though he was mentally gone and not himself, somewhere in his subconscious his love for me shielded me from the staining imagery of him "like this".

It is in this moment I feel his deep sadness, shame, and love all together at once.

As I walk away, I don't love him less, I somehow love him more.

Enrika Greathouse is a creative entrepreneur and community builder. As the founder of Small Gorilla Marketing, she crafts innovative campaigns that blend art with storytelling. As the Community Advocate for the Story Republic, she champions connection through shared narratives. Through her workshops, writing, and speaking engagements, Enrika explores how play, creativity, and human connection catalyze growth. No matter what she's up to, her passion lies in cultivating spaces where people can connect, create, and thrive together.

The Hustle

When I was in the 4th grade, my older brother held a disco party at our house. He was in the 8th grade and invited his group of friends.

I was boy crazy, enamored of my popular brother, and beside myself at the prospect of having all the cool kids in my own home.

The first to arrive was a quiet tall boy named Billy. He wore the same polyester shirt my brother had on—causing quite a stir between the two of them.

I'm pretty sure my younger sister and I were banned from the festivities (because I don't remember much after the first arrivals), but Billy took pity on us. We were desperate to be included. So, he taught us *The Hustle* before the party started.

Da da da da da da tee dee da ta . . . Do the Hustle!

Maybe he was looking to avoid the polyester showdown with my brother. Maybe he was shy, and grateful to break the ice with an easier audience. Maybe he was just a natural born teacher—someone who saw another person's eagerness to learn and shared what he knew. And maybe he was—even then—a natural born leader, creating a sense of belonging and possibility as he taught us the steps.

I should ask him. I married that boy eighteen years later.

Anne Roche loves stories—hearing them, reading them, sharing them, listening for what's underneath them. She uses the power of stories in her work as a life leadership coach, the writer of her Fire and Light *newsletter, and a podcaster. Anne loves being part of a writing community celebrating storytellers and storytelling. You can learn about her coaching at annerochecoaching.com.*

Unleashed

On my way to pick up Zara from school, I receive a call from her.

"Can you meet me at the front doors instead of the back?"

Her voice is muffled, sounding like a mix of tears and mucus lodged somewhere between eyes and nose. I can tell she's been crying.

She opens the car door and drops into the passenger seat. But when I examine the face I've known for seventeen years, I cannot find my child. The one I know is bubbly, energetic, and lets encumbrances roll. The one next to me is a stranger, uncharacteristically void of expression.

"What happened?" I ask.

"I just wanna go home," she says, eyes fixed on the windshield, body still.

I ask more questions but all I get is silence.

This is about yesterday. I know it.

Early in the academic year, Zara and a tiny group of concerned schoolmates began work on an initiative requiring administrative approval. Over many months, they engaged in long negotiations with staff, navigating an alarmingly opaque, mismanaged, and, at times, biased process.

Repeated roadblocks—inconsistent with the school's commitments to student advocacy, social justice, and the core value of *beloved community*—had left Zara and other student leaders reeling. For people of color in particular, the discriminatory policies and practices highlighted by the process damaged their sense of belonging.

To articulate their mounting frustrations, the students requested a meeting with their head of school and, a day ago, met with senior administrators, including Rob, a longtime ally.

Their advocacy was compelling. The head of school commended them on their leadership and finally gave them permission to move forward with the initiative. With less than a week before summer break, the decision delivered a long-awaited, timely win.

Overnight, something has clearly changed.

"*What's going on?*" I ask Zara, with deepening concern.

After prolonged silence, she relents. "I met Rob right before you came."

"Did he change his mind?"

"No," Zara says. "It's the school. They want to pause to figure stuff out. Something about they're '*not ready*' to do this because . . . complications. Sensitivities. Bullshit basically."

"That's ridiculous." I say, "They've had months—"

"And, they want us to pause our work too."

"*Why?*"

"He doesn't know," she says, ripe with grief. "Mama can we please just go home?"

My head is spinning. Still, I start to drive.

Today's stonewalling is a devastating blow. I too feel distressed at the school's failures to do right by students on this issue, and now, a reneged agreement.

We complete the ride home like injured birds with clipped wings, swallowed by songless silence. Once on the driveway, I push the clutch into park.

But Zara remains seated, her hollowed cheeks glistening with lines of saltwater. Below them, her hand rests over her heart.

"What's the matter?" I ask.

"I feel heavy," she says, pressing on her chest.

She is seventeen, healthy, and well-liked at school. Her chest should not feel heavy. Though her advocacy had manifested many hair-yanking moments, I assumed that her resilient nature would neutralize the blows.

Now, I sense my error. Losses, when accumulated, inevitably take their toll. A tangle of heat at the base of my throat begins to rise.

"It's ok," I say, tightening my grip on the steering wheel. "Let's do some breathing."

This time, she responds immediately with a nod.

"Alright. Together. In. Two, three. Out. Two, three, four, five . . ."

Her chest swells, then collapses.

"Not the chest," I say, gently. "Remember?"

I watch as she stops, then restarts after some adjustments. *She does remember.*

For several minutes, we breathe, ballooning and
deflating our bellies, intent on restoring our aching,
ailing hearts. Like this, we settle into a slow,
synchronous rhythm.

"I'm *so* tired mama," she says, dropping tears again.

A high-spirited, chatty teen, with no words or will to
speak, struggles to breathe with the protracted effort
of an old woman. This is the impact of a system with
no incentive to take ethical stands.

In the past, I might have felt outraged. Right now
though, I register only gratitude. A child's
exhaustion, after all, is easier to remedy than their
despair.

———————————

After dinner, Zara sits in the family room finishing
year-end assignments. Just before eleven, she folds
her computer shut. Her eyes are red and swollen from
the day's drain.

I know she's spent. I also know that lessons learned
from personal experience have far greater impact
than those relayed by others. Yet, fearing that she's
too attached, I feel compelled to speak.

"Can we debrief on today?" I ask, scanning her face for even a glint of willingness.

She nods.

"In this kind of work," I start, "we have no control over outcomes. Or timing. Change could happen next month. Or next year. Or never. So . . ." I search for words that can bring perspective without extinguishing her spirit. "We engage with hope. But without expectation of results."

"I know," she says.

"And, we *have* to take breaks to rest. To repair."

I pause, curious to know her reaction.

"I'm realizing," she says finally, "that compartmentalizing is hard for me. So . . . *yes*, I need a break."

With that, she stands. Her words convey a sadness that I hope doesn't signal resignation.

"Mama, can I sleep with you again tonight?"

It had been years since Zara last made this request. Now, she has done it two nights in a row.

As a child, she migrated to my bed virtually every night. Eventually, she learned to sleep in her own room, so well in fact, that now, if ever I ask to do a sleepover—for old time's sake—she says she prefers her own bed.

But tonight, I'm the one who's not keen. She's been sick for some time—no longer contagious I'm sure—but as someone who, post-pandemic, still feels cautious of illness, the instinct for self-preservation is hard to snuff.

"Sure," I say, then half-joke, "but you can't breathe on me."

She steps forward and circles her arms around my waist. We lean into each other gently—both aware of our tender states—in a slow, long embrace.

"Can you play the prayer from last night, too?"

"Of course," I say, surprised by this request even more than the first. She never asks to listen to prayer recitations.

Zara falls asleep within minutes, long before the prayer ends. When her breathing deepens, I start to slide away, looking to get a drink of water.

But as I pivot to swing my legs over the edge of the bed, her arm shoots out to grab mine.

I turn toward her to notice her eyes shut, breathing still audible. Lowering my head back onto the pillow, I place my palm on her hair and whisper.

"Mama's right here, Zara. Sleep."

I wake the next morning before the alarm, teetering on the edge of the bed, face to the nightstand, back to Zara. The night was fretful, marked with repeated wakings to distance myself from her while she kept seeking proximity.

This morning, maternal instinct prevails. I rotate to face her, minding my movements to avoid shaking the bed, until I have a clear view.

She is sleeping on her back, head turned toward me. Her skin is aglow with lines of early light slipping through the white wooden window blinds. I marvel at the serenity of slumbering children, no matter their age. It never fails to evoke the divine.

As I absorb the rush of her beauty, my awareness of her *being* grows until it becomes impossible to ignore the parallel presence of her profound setbacks, losses, and pains. Despite her young age and many privileges, they too exist. They too contribute to the fullness of her humanity.

I consider the immense dismay of working for months on something that might disappear into the annals of administrative purgatory, all because the adults in the room can't face their discomforts and, instead, attempt to disguise them as placations.

We don't want to silence you. Don't worry. It's a temporary pause.

I lie with my own discomfort, feeling the familiar pain of obstacles stifling social change. One after another, they erode hope for justice. They kill our trust. Stirred by the possibility of these troubling outcomes, my sadness, in all its blazing colours, rises with the morning sun.

I spent the night retreating, inch by inch, from a child whose wound, layered and complex, is still so raw that the extent of its harm remains unknown. How will this experience shape her? In considering its impact, I am infused with a tenderness so intense, it sparks a sudden, inexplicable desire to move closer.

Lifting the edge of my pillow, I drag it a few inches toward Zara, then extend my hand to graze the bright yellow sleeve concealing her right shoulder. But something feels unsettled.

I drop my fingers an inch or so, enough to settle

on her sleeve without disturbing her arm underneath. Still, something's not right.

So, I slide my pillow forward once again, body following, until I'm close enough to wrap my palm around her arm firmly.

Here, finally, I find stillness. I imagine an invisible line stemming from my heart, moving down my arm, past my wrist, across my palm, through my fingertips onto Zara's sleeve, passing over her chest, and ending, finally, in her heart. *We are connected.*

That's when it begins: a piercing pain on the left side of my chest. At first, I think nothing of it. Sometimes when distressed, I feel a similar, fleeting sting. But when it fails to subside after many minutes, I wonder if today, it might mean something different.

I maintain a steady hold on Zara's arm, while inside my chest, the sharpness grows.

My heart hurts. Yet, with our bodies connected, heart to heart, I wonder: whose suffering is it? Could the heaviness in her chest be transferring to mine?

Surrendering myself to the possibility, I close my eyes and imagine drawing the universe of sorrows and injustices, past and present, out from her aching heart.

A spiritual teacher of mine recently revealed the truth about love: to think of it as a feeling is to short-sell it.

Love is a life force unleashed onto the universe by God, or whichever other power one believes to be the source of all sentient beings. Like an immutable flame, that same force burns in the deepest part of all hearts.

As I consider this wisdom, a new pain arises in the same vicinity as the first, but on my back instead of in my chest. Unlike the first though, it leaves within seconds after it arrives. And once it does, both the pains vanish altogether.

Startled, I release my grip on Zara's arm. The flinch, though subtle, disturbs her just enough to rouse her from sleep. Slowly, she awakens.

In the past, she might have stretched her limbs emphatically, punctuating the full-body yawn with a verbal exclamation. She might have smiled or quipped with signature dry humor.

She doesn't do these things today. Instead, she lies facing me, silent, peaceful, still. After all she's experienced over the last many weeks, it will take longer for the bubbly to return.

But her eyes are back.

Between intermittent sweeps of her thick black lashes, their clarity grows. They have returned, brimming with firepower. Safe within them, the bright force of nature that nobody, no system, however unjust, can smother, lives on.

I savour the peacefulness of this moment, wishing it could cradle us both just a bit longer. But it's past eight already and she can't be late for school.

"Time to get up, Zara," I say softly.

To my relief, she does.

Sabah Mirza discovered the beauty of words through Urdu ghazals, Sufi poetry, and 'gupshup' with her Nani. Later, she learned that words woven with intent can reveal the human condition, build bridges, ease pain. As a heart-centered advisor, facilitator, and writer grounded in the ethics of human worth and dignity, she creates stories and workshops to build empathy, connection, and belonging. Sabah draws inspiration from five decades of personal, professional, and spiritual journeying, a BSME from MIT, and an MBA from Stanford University. She's currently writing a story collection about wisdom unearthed from proximity. Learn more at sabahmirza.com

Love Stories

One.

My friend Duane and I call each other a few times a week. He is ninety-three years old. We were talking a few days ago, and he brought up Lonnie, his late wife. He said when Lonnie was on the phone with her cousin Kat, they laughed and laughed. Lonnie's laugh didn't sound like that when she spoke with anyone else. Duane always knew when Kat was on the other line.

Two.

Walking into the kitchen for the first night of a restaurant job. Jimmy introduced me to Jan. She said, "Do I know you?" Her eyes looked like planets. I stood still. Smitten.

Three.

Thirty years later, Jan and I took a Black Taxi tour in Belfast, Ireland. The driver passionately told us the

history of the violent conflict between the Loyalists
and Republicans. We saw different neighborhoods,
and historical murals, and visited "peace walls" built
of brick and barbed wire to separate people in hopes
of keeping violence down. On each side of the peace
walls were memorials with pictures of women, men,
children, and animals who died in the conflict.
At one wall the driver wept. He walked away and lit a
cigarette.

Four.

Valentine's Day. A national call to express and
acknowledge someone you love. The Valentine's cards
I got when I was in grade school made me feel liked
and excited! In my early twenties, the day was a
reminder of what wasn't in my life. I felt ashamed.
Unlovable. My cynic says it's an advertising scheme
that fuels spending and makes crappy chocolate and
stinky perfume pale symbols of love. Even though I
have a partnership with Jan that my twenty-
something self could only dream of. And even though,
some days, my heart is as tender as a seven-year-
old's.

Five.

Love is more than I can grasp. But a symbol of love
lives inside me, beating, as if to say love you,
love you,
love you.

As someone who is often moved to tears by the artistry that animates music, cooking, and photography, Dave Lewis writes stories that invoke an appreciation for beauty and celebrate an earnest pursuit of love. These are stories that his readers find to be moving, too. He resides in Minneapolis, Minnesota, with his wife Jan Elftmann.

Ants

Ants have invaded my kitchen. It's kind of impressive, since I live on the second floor.

I stagger into the kitchen, in a fever, to find ants all over the sink. Almost without thinking about it, I react. I turn on the water and flush them all away, refill my glass and head back to bed. I've quipped for years now that 'live and let live stops inside the house'. Over the next few hours, racked with fever and thirst—and guilt—I am disturbed by my capacity for casual violence.

The next morning, the sink is heaving with ants again. A shiver runs down my back. The glass I was about to rinse, clicks on the countertop when my hand drops. As my shadow passes over them, some of the ants flinch away, running for cover beneath the edge of the glass bowl I left to soak the night before.

One is carrying a crumb valiantly up the side of the
sink. Around each tiny fragment of food debris, they
feast. I can feel their desperate joy in their waving
feet. They do not fight over food. They seem, rather,
to take comfort in the presence of the others. Turning
my head shifts my hand, and I slop some water,
which washes a few unlucky ones away. Their legs
wave in panic as they are swept down the drain. My
eyes fill with tears and I flick the tap off. One ant
crawls free of the tide and stops, exhausted. I do not
see it move again. I feel sick.

I just . . . I just don't want to kill them and I don't
know what to do.

One ant scrabbles for purchase, skirting the lake of a
water drop, trying to find a path to safety. Another
runs to shelter in the fatal, deceptive darkness of the
plughole. I panic. I grab a knife lying on the draining
board and tap the handgrip a few times on the metal
surface. *Tap! Tap! Tap!* The sound sends it scurrying
away. I keep tapping, muttering under my breath,

"Just get out of the sink. I don't want to kill you. Just
go away, for God's sake!"

I repeat my tapping whenever they slow, driven by
the sight or smell of food to risk disaster. I regard
them with compassion and mild revulsion. In less
than a minute, they evacuate to the comparative

safety of the countertop. I turn on the tap and fill my water glass, relieved that I haven't had to perform a massacre, and head back to bed on shaky legs.

I repeat this encounter several times over the next couple of days. It might be my imagination, but they seem to respond more quickly, like they're learning. By the third day I am well enough to properly scrub down the countertop and sink area. The ants are less active when I'm able to keep the kitchen immaculate, washing each cup or plate as soon as it is used.

They begin to forage further afield. I open the pantry door and find a street party happening inside a bag of icing sugar: it's inside a sealed storage crate, which has sprung an unnoticed hole. Beside it a brand-new storage jar from the dollar store must have an imperfect seal: a dozen ants have smothered, drowned in the fatal softness of cornflour. One just quivers on the rim, when I grab the jar, intending rescue, it falls into snowy oblivion. I weep for my clumsiness, then a box of cereal slips from my hand and crushes a dozen more.

Out of options, I wash the sugar-blissed ants away. At least it was quick, and their bellies were full, I comfort myself. To assuage my guilt, a little, I leave the storage crate near the crack in the floor so the rest of the ants can depart in safety.

"Want me to wipe out the rest of the pantry?" my friend offers. I fear she will wipe the ants away too.

"No," I say. "Everything is sealed now; they'll lose interest and be gone by tomorrow."

She looks at me like I am crazy. I suspect she won't be coming over to eat anytime soon. That evening the pantry is clear. Armed by advice from the Internet, I wipe all the surfaces to erase any scent trails they've left.

Next, I discover they've invaded the kitchen bin. I harden my heart and tie up the bag—ants and all— and chuck it down the bin chute. I find myself wondering when the bins will be emptied. I'm haunted by thoughts of them, down there in the dark: suffocating, gasping for air, or starving slowly, searching for a way out that does not exist. I picture their confusion, they won't understand what is going on, why this event has happened to them.

The ants' imagined confusion is echoed in the news, which I cannot watch or read, in my enfeebled state, but which is almost impossible to completely avoid. This is not political and there is no malice in my actions, but for the ants I am nonetheless a cataclysmic disaster. They are the civilian casualties I am willing to accept. My lack of malice makes no difference to their experience.

I increase my vigilance. All food waste goes into a
sealed Tupperware container on the countertop. I
wipe all spills immediately. I pray, literally, that they
never find their way into the dishwasher.

They invade the bin again, lured by cardboard take-
away containers. There are no leftovers, but thanks to
the famine I have enforced, the grease and salt
residue is incentive enough. A narrow tide of hungry
ants stretches from the crack in the floor and up the
side of the bin. There are hundreds, maybe thousands
of them in the light spilling from the bathroom at 2
a.m.

I can't save them all, but I will do what I can. I get my
trusty knife and seat myself on a stool, then
begin *Tap! Tap! Tap!* on the side of the bin. The first
exodus of the fleeing, sounding the alarm, meets
the incoming ants. Most reverse, spreading a wave of
retreat. The survivors of previous disasters are
vigilant and leave at the first sign of impending doom.
But ants are civilians. No sergeants hurry the
laggards. A minority continues against the flow. Is it
innocence or desperation that drives them? Some
retreat to the bottom of the bin bag, sealing their fate.
It takes almost twenty minutes of tapping, until
around two thirds of the ants have made it out. I tie

the bin bag tightly over the casualties, hoping it will
be quick.

Stray ants sometimes end up in distant locations,
carried on my clothing. I find one on my pillow when I
roll onto it; it attacks me in a futile effort to defend
itself. Half asleep, I scratch at an itch and crush it. I
don't feel so bad about that one, since my cheek is
itching and smarting. Revenge is more numbing than
sweet, it would seem, I am sickened by the
realisation.

One ant has made it all the way to the bathroom basin.
Whenever my shadow passes, it hides behind the soap
dispenser. I try to lure it onto a scrap of paper, to take
it back to its fellows, but it flees in terror. I give up
when continuing to chase it feels too cruel. Can ants
have heart attacks? I guess it has learned the hard way
that walking onto surfaces with a different texture
can have negative consequences. It will find its way
out, I tell myself. Ants get everywhere. But each time I
use the bathroom, it hasn't yet.

It was moving slower last night. So was I, exhausted
by my first full day up and about again. I've promised
myself that this morning I will figure out how to catch
it and take it back to its friends. I can't bear to watch
it starve, alone, adrift on a desert of white vitreous
porcelain.

"Everything just wants to live," my twin brother told me, as he neared death himself.

I corner the bathroom ant between my scrap of paper and the tap. When I set the paper down by the ants emerging from the crack in the floor, 'my' ant rushes through the stream of its fellows. It seems relieved as it disappears, heading home. I cry for joy.

I've never liked ants, have always been a bit creeped out by them. I'd rather not have ants in my house. But that no longer seems a good enough reason to kill them. I never imagined I could care so much about such alien creatures, but this past week I have become painfully aware of what we have in common.

And I wonder, is this a kind of love?

Michelle Spencer hails from Melbourne, Australia. She is a writer, philosopher and sometime entrepreneur. At heart she is a magpie collector of unusual insights, people and other shiny delights. Her goals include coaxing wisdom from knowledge and experience, and becoming more herself. In addition to her Substack newsletter Armchair Rebel: Chronic Reflections Inspired by Life in the Slow Lane, *she is working on a memoir,* The Geometry of Grief: Life Lessons from the Death Trade.

"Love has nothing to do with what
you are expecting to get—only
with what you are expecting to
give—which is everything."

-Katherine Hepburn

PART 2

Love is:

*the twists
and turns.*

Mole Chicken

By the time the Mole Chicken arrives at the table, the sauce has already started to coagulate.

The chicken is dry. Dry as a stone.

After eating a few bites, I can't continue for fear of choking. The fear that someone will need to do the Heimlich Maneuver on me to open my airway is real.

I came here to fill up after a long hike. This is supposed to be a nice restaurant. I normally finish all the food on my plate, but not this Mole Chicken. I don't send the meal back because that's not something I do. With me, a restaurant has one shot to produce a good meal and no more. I figure if the chef doesn't care enough about his patrons to make a delicious meal every time, it's not my job to force him to do so.

I nibble at the rice and beans. I eat all of the chips and salsa but I decide not to order more because I don't want to consume additional empty calories.

I wonder if the chef here just settles for sub-par quality, produces something, and isn't concerned when the plates come back full of food. I imagine him showing no awareness or caring about his art.

I'm tired. My stomach is growling. I feel hunger pangs as I leave the restaurant.

I trudge for blocks until something unexpected catches my eye.

At first, I think it's a mirage. As I get closer the place comes into focus. I see that it's an ice cream shop.

The owner, Dave, is very welcoming. He offers me many samples to taste and tells me the stories behind some of the more noteworthy ones.

Dad's Famous Mint Chip is inspired by his father. He too is an ice cream maker. And introduced Dave to blending handmade artisan ice cream.

And Mom's Cranberry Relish Ice tastes like the cranberry sauce his Mom makes at Thanksgiving.

I decide on Dad's Famous Mint Chip. Handmade with garden fresh spearmint leaves. And rich dark chocolate flakes mixed in. It's creamy, smooth and just the right amount of sweetness.

The evening could have been a disaster if I had let the Mole Chicken dominate. But somehow, I opened up to the possibility of one final delight to end the day on a positive note.

In my notebook, I write about the breathtaking sunset and the beautiful hike. And about Dave—his generosity, kindness, love and caring for people, the love of his craft, and the fortuitous discovery of his yummy ice cream treats.

Susan E. draws cartoons and tells stories for enjoyment and to entertain friends and family. She's constantly on the lookout for moments she wants to use to craft stories and illustrations. For Susan, moments are as ubiquitous as gulls snatching sandwiches at the seashore. But if she doesn't scribble these moments on scrap paper when she notices them, they may fly away. Susan's stories and drawings frequently feature animals, plants, and creatures. Her pursuits also include hiking, open water swimming, half marathons, and consuming massive quantities of chocolate.

If You Really Knew Me

It's early spring in 2008, and I'm sitting in a crowd watching a local author, Mike Robbins, talk about his newly-released book. As part of his talk, he presences an activity he calls the "Iceberg."[2] In this exercise, what you do is take the chance to "drop the water line" in how you share about yourself and let people learn a bit about who you really are.

As he demonstrates it, there are close to a hundred pairs of eyes on him, in rapt attention, mine included.

First, he says something like, "If you really knew me, you'd know I'm super grateful to be here speaking to you all today."

---

[2] The "Iceberg Exercise" was developed by the founders of ChallengeDay and is illustrated in their book *Be The Hero You've Been Waiting For* by Yvonne and Rich Dutra-St. John. Learn about their extraordinary anti-bullying organization by visiting ChallengeDay.org

After that, he says, "If you really, really knew me, you'd know I'm married, we have a two-year-old daughter, and we're excited we have another one on the way."

When he shares that second one, I think, "Oh, that's an odd and unexpected detail. We're here to learn about his book, not his personal life." I also notice I like knowing this about him.

And then he says, "If you really, really, really knew me, you'd know that I'm actually kind of nervous and scared to be up here speaking to you all right now. What if what I say doesn't make sense, or you're not interested in hearing about my book?"

This last one stops me in my tracks. From my perspective, he's doing a great job holding everyone's attention by seeming super relaxed and confident while telling interesting stories and anecdotes. Instead, he's admitting he's nervous, just like I certainly would be.

I never forgot that moment.

A few years later, I end up working with Mike in a coaching relationship. As part of our work, he recommends I take some personal growth and development courses to help get to the source of what truly matters to me—personally and professionally.

From doing that work, I create who I truly want to be

for myself and others is the possibility of love and connection.

Another few years go by, and I'm at a networking lunch. It's a small group and we're sitting in a beautiful atrium on a lovely spring day. There are white tablecloths, everyone looks spiffy, and we're all on our best behavior. It's your typical cast of characters:

Real Estate Agent
Wealth Planner
Web Designer
Estate Attorney
Interior Decorator
Insurance Agent

You get the picture. And then there's me.

My coaching assignment that week, based on what I said I wanted, is to stand inside my possibility of being a space for love and connection, no matter what. When I arrive at the lunch, I am committed to staying true to my assignment.

As we go around the table to introduce ourselves, it is clear, due to where I am sitting, my turn will be last. As each person shares their tried-and-true elevator speech and ideal client summary, my anxiety is ramping up. In my mind, the conversation is going something like this, "What do I do, chicken out and hide behind my elevator speech? Or do I stick to my commitment and be real?"

It's finally my turn, and with my heart pounding, yet somehow outwardly managing to remain cool as a cucumber, I take a deep breath and let them know I'm going to take a slightly different approach. I presence the "Iceberg Exercise" to them.

And then I demonstrate it:

"If you really knew me, you'd know I'm passionate about my business of creating life story videos with people."

"If you really, really knew me, you'd know that what I love most about my work is experiencing the impact my full presence and deep listening has on the people I'm honored to interview."

"If you really, really, really knew me, you'd know in my younger days I'd rarely felt seen, heard, or noticed. It's such a gift to myself that I'm able to give that to others."

I can tell everyone isn't exactly sure what to think about this new tack I've taken. But I'm already all in, so I request we now spend the rest of my allotted time going around the table with each person sharing something that truly matters to them, personal or professional.

Part of me is terrified that they are all thinking I am nuts.

But one by one, they lean in and share something personal about themselves. As we get to the third or fourth person, I notice the shoulders of the wealth planner have relaxed. The interior designer is tapping her cheek as she gazes off into the distance to collect her thoughts while wrapping up her share. The brows of the real estate agent are knit with curiosity as he pitches a bit forward in his seat while asking a follow-up question. I'm somewhat awestruck to see each person open up like one of the beautiful spring blossoms on the trees lining the sidewalk just outside our atrium. The energy moves from that nervous, somewhat obligatory "when's this lunch going to be over" vibe to a warm and relaxed table of nine people connecting on a deep level and seeing their shared humanity. Long gone are thoughts of them thinking I'm nuts.

I never forgot about that.

If you really knew me, you'd know I'm grateful I had the courage to be my true self that day.

If you really, really knew me, you'd know that what I learned was that by being my true self and stepping outside of a box I never wanted to be in, I gave others permission to do the same.

If you really, really, really knew me, you'd know that being the possibility of love and connection still terrifies me to this day. But maybe, just maybe, if I keep showing you my heart, you'll be willing to show me yours, too.

April Bell is the founder at Tree of Life Legacies, a storytelling and wisdom-keeping project based in the San Francisco Bay Area. She helps people find and tell the origin stories behind their values, often on video. April spent her early days listening to stories from whichever elder neighbor would have her. In 2023, her story-mining process became My Life in Paragraphs: Find and Tell Your Stories, *her first book, delighting people who love storytelling but are daunted by writing. She is the co-creator of the iPhone app, StoryCatcher® Pro. Learn more about her story work at aprilbell.com*

Better Together

I was sitting across from Carla at her kitchen table, tears rolling softly down her cheeks. Our hands warmed by mugs of tea; our bellies full of the brownies I had made that morning.

Over the years I had seen Carla face more than her fair share of heartache. One failed relationship after another. And not one of them, her fault.

Her children were young when her marriage ended. She'd done everything she could to hold her family together, but Gary had wanted to drink.

After the breakup, Carla met Adam, a single dad with a daughter the same age as hers. He seemed great, but it turned out his "past" drug habit wasn't.

Personal trainer Peter lived a healthy lifestyle. Over the phone, he would woo Carla declaring love and adoration. But in person, he was not a man of his word.

After her kids left home, she met Robert. His caring had quickly morphed into control. The only exit was out of town.

It was now twenty years since her marriage had ended, yet despite all that she had gone through, Carla hadn't given up.

"Am I asking too much?"

"No, Carla. More than anyone I know, you deserve to find love. Proper love."

This upcoming cruise would be a much-needed break from a demanding job, a chance to get away from it all, and maybe I suggested, where she would meet "the man of her dreams".

She smiled, wiping the mascara streaks from under her eyes, "That would be perfect—just as long as he's based in Auckland and not Timbuktu!"

I called her the week she got back.

"How was the trip?"

"It was wonderful. So relaxing. I should have done it sooner."

After she shared the highlights . . . I couldn't wait to ask.

"And . . . love?"

"Sadly, nothing to report. It doesn't matter though; I had a great time."

Three weeks later she responded to a text saying she was away for the weekend and would call me later.

My 'potential news' radar spiked . . . a weekend away?

She rang two days later. "I have some news . . ."

"Oooo, I had a feeling you did—tell me!"

"Well, I did meet a guy on the cruise. We were on the same team at a quiz night. We had a fun time but nothing more.

My friend Sue rang when I got back, and like you, she asked me if I had met anyone, so I mentioned 'Quiz' guy because she was insistent that *'There must have been someone!'*

I only knew his first name. It's Oliver. As soon as she heard his name, she started asking all these questions. Where was he from? What colour was his hair, his eyes? How tall? Could I see any tattoos? I answered what I could and then she let out this almighty squeal.

It turns out she and Oliver have been friends for over twenty years! She kept raving about what a great guy he is and insisted she connect us.

He lives in Raglan, not Auckland, but at least it's only two hours away. Since exchanging numbers we've had a couple of dates. He's been up to see me and last weekend I visited him. He's so lovely—we talk for hours . . .”

“Wow, that's wonderful news! And amazing! So, let me get this straight—you didn't have any way of contacting each other? You didn't exchange last names or phone numbers or anything?”

“No. I only knew his first name. We got on well at the quiz night, but I didn't see him again.

“Oh, and get this . . . he hadn't even planned on going on that cruise. A family member pulled out and Oliver decided to go at the last minute.”

“What an incredible start to a love story. YOUR love story! Talk about serendipity! I'm so happy for you!”

Later when I shared Carla's news, my friend Anne said, “I love it! It reminds me of the importance of saying things out loud to other people. We truly are better together but only when we share our hearts generously.”

Anne's words struck a chord. If Carla hadn't shared this seemingly unimportant story, all that the serendipity angels were trying to line up would never have come to pass.

It made me think of my tendency to hold things close to my heart, to not share too much, and to have "nothing to report."

How had I thwarted the acts of angels by not sharing my heart courageously or generously?

Carla had always done both. And this time had seeded a beautiful love story.

Jacquie Landeman doesn't have a job title but has a much-loved J.O.B. in a small finance company in Auckland, New Zealand, working for a team that inspires and encourages innovation and out-of-the-box thinking. Her passion lies in the customer experience. Beyond work, Jacquie volunteers as a budgeting coach for Christians Against Poverty; runs a women's group; and organizes street parties. For the sheer delight of creative discovery, in the supportive company of like-minded others, Jacquie enjoys being a member of The Story Republic, *practicing the art of storytelling while also honing her communication skills at Toastmasters.*

Love is Seafood

In the summer of 1954, long before I arrived, my father and 8-year-old brother waded in the salty mud-bottom cove of Green Bridge, Newport, RI.

The sun was high and bright in the sky, but the water remained cool, sending shivers up my brother Ric's spine as he stood chest-deep, digging by hand for Quahogs (co-hog, kwo-hawg). Recognizing Ric's discomfort, my father, ever the practical man, sent him back to shore with the two overflowing bushel baskets, each floating in the center of an inner tube. The baskets bobbed gently as Ric, eager to escape the cold, made his way toward the shoreline where our trusty Willys Jeep waited.

As you imagine Ric trudging through the water, I'd like you to take a moment to get a close look at the clam they were gathering—the Quahog. Picture it by placing your hands together as if you're praying. Now, form a cup or bowl with your hands, and close it, bring your thumbs together. The small volume of air in the palms of your hands represents the meaty inside of the Quahog. Your thumbs, touching side-by-side, act as the opposing lips of its hard shell. Now, create a hinge where your pinkies are, and imagine your thumbs opening slightly, just enough for the Quahog's feeding snout to pass through.

The Clam doesn't typically open these shell lips very wide except when safely feeding under the mud. The shell's tight seal keeps the Quahog safe from small predators on the ocean floor. When feeding, it slowly pushes its long, tubular mouth—almost like an elephant's trunk—out through the small opening, siphoning water and nutrients. When disturbed, the clam will s-l-o-w-l-y retract its snout and close its lips. Once closed, those shell lips are impossible for the bare hand to open.

To extract the sweet meat, the Clam must be baked or steamed until the shell willingly opens, offering its bounty. My father knew this well; on that summer day in 1954, he was determined to bring home a feast. Ric, now standing at the shoreline, lingered near the Jeep, likely trying to shake off the chill. But before settling in, he heard our father shouting from the water.

"Ric! Ric! Get the screwdriver! Get-the-Screwdriver!"

My father's voice was strained, almost panicked, as he fought through the waist-deep water, his body creating waves as he pushed forward.

"Screwdriver! Screwdriver!"

Startled, Ric grabbed the tool from the Jeep and turned just in time to see our father, with a pained expression on his otherwise loving face, reach the shore. Dad snatched the screwdriver and, in a moment of modesty, turned his back to Ric before dropping his swim trunks to his ankles.

Ric watched, puzzled, as Dad struggled with something hidden from view. Then it dawned on him—Dad had found a mother lode and had been stuffing more clams into his pants. But one of those clams had a surprise of its own—it had securely attached itself to Dad's foreskin.

My father, desperate to free himself, gritted his teeth as he tried to pry open the shell with the screwdriver. When that failed, he flipped the tool around and used the handle as a hammer, each strike sending a dull thud through the quiet afternoon air until the shell finally shattered.

Relieved from the lips of his unwanted friend, Dad, with his swim trunks comically at his ankles, laden with clams, turned to Ric, his voice softening despite the pain and tears in his eyes.

"Now, let that be a lesson. Don't be greedy."

Ric nodded solemnly, his young face a mixture of shock and understanding, the lesson searing into his mind. "Don't be greedy," Dad repeated, this time with a weary smile.

Just prior to the pandemic, John Braman (62) converted his in-ground swimming pool in Encinitas, California, to a natural pond with fish, plants, muck, dragonflies, and all that nature continues to offer. The story above transpired at Ocean Drive, Green Bridge, Newport, Rhode Island. Ric (77) a grandfather, helicopter and fixed wing pilot, skydiver, and otherwise nice human, chuckled when he learned this story would be published.

Love in the Most Unlikely Places

It's June, but it's already 98 degrees Fahrenheit in the shade, which is unusually hot for spring in New England.

I'm at an ice cream event with my husband, Bill. He bought tickets to a fundraiser to support cancer research and patient care.

It's not a big event. There are twelve, maybe fourteen ice cream vendors with booths erected in a parking lot adjacent to Gillette Stadium, where the New England Patriots play football.

Each vendor has four to five flavors of ice cream to sample. I've decided that I'm going to eat my way through the 60+ flavors. That shouldn't be too difficult because each sample is only about three ounces.

I flash my rubber bracelet at each booth. It indicates I have an upgraded ticket that allows me to move to the front of the line.

After eight cups or so, I begin to feel queasy.

I tell Bill I need to sit down. He finds a tiny patch of shade under a tree. As I settle against the oak tree, I feel worse in less than a minute.

I need to use the restroom.

There's a line of portable toilets not too far from where we're sitting. I stumble over, step inside, and close the door. As I begin to undo the button on my shorts, the stifling heat overcomes me. It feels like it's 180 degrees in here. I'm afraid that I'm going to pass out.

The fear of that happening sends me frantically bounding outside.

A handwashing station is set up directly across from the portable toilets. Grabbing onto the edge, I scream Bill's name three times with all the strength I can muster. He finally hears me and rushes over to the wash station.

I'm standing there with my head resting on my hands as I stare down at the ground.

"Are you ok?" Bill asks.

"No," I whisper.

Out of the corner of my eye, I see a groundskeeper's broom stop near me.

He asks Bill, "Do you need help?"

Bill says, "Yes, she's not feeling well." There's fear in his voice. The groundskeeper goes to get help.
A few minutes later, a flurry of uniforms surrounds me. EMTs and police officers hold me up and guide me back to the patch of shade under the tree.

They help me sit down. One of them spritzes my face with water.

I mumble to Bill, "My head." I feel mist spraying on my head.

"No Bill. More water," I insist. Bill empties his bottle of water on my head. The ringing in my ears stops, the fog begins to lift, and I start to breathe easier.

One of the guys in uniform asks me, "Do you know where you are?"

All I can whisper is, "Ice cream."

He chuckles and says, "I think you've had enough!" He speaks into his walkie-talkie, requesting a golf cart to take us back to Bill's car.

When the golf cart arrives, two police officers help me
up from the ground and settle me in the cart next to
Bill. As the driver starts to pull off, he tells Bill to hold
onto me so I don't fall out. I guess I still look a little
green!

I close my eyes and lean against Bill's shoulder as the
golf cart speeds towards the parking lot. What a
spectacle I am. I can't take a little sun and ice cream!

The driver stops the golf cart a few feet from the car.
Bill gets out, and I see him and a police officer looking
into the trunk of the car. Bill removes a blanket and
spreads it on the passenger's seat.

Bill takes my hand as I step from the cart. I tell the
driver I don't feel well and I want to use the restroom.
He tells us there's a hotel nearby or maybe we can go
to a restaurant.

I don't understand what the driver means when he
says, "You can take care of that there."

Impatiently, I ask, "Isn't there any place closer we
can go? Inside the stadium?" He says it's locked, but
he can lead us to a hospital on the other side of the
building.

In two minutes, we're at the door of the emergency
room.

Bill helps me into a wheelchair and pushes it to the
check-in desk. After I give the receptionist my

medical information, a nurse wheels me to the waiting room. Just as she's about to leave, I ask her to take me to the washroom.

She wheels me down the corridor to an individual restroom. My head is less foggy. I feel steadier on my feet. She allows me to go inside alone. The sensor turns the light on automatically as I enter and lock the door.

I stand in front of the toilet and shakily pull down my pants.

OMG! I had no idea of the mess I had in my shorts, my underwear, and down my legs. I try to empty as much as I can into the toilet, but it's getting everywhere . . . on the toilet seat, on my hands, spilling onto the floor.

I squish my shorts into a ball and drop them into the sink. I run the water and try not to clog the drain. It's an actual shit show!

What was I thinking? I'm lactose intolerant. I have no business eating that much ice cream in this heat. But Bill was excited about coming to the event, and it's for a worthy cause, so I agreed.

I need help! Just as I crack open the door to call Bill, I see him raise his fist to knock. He steps inside. The look of horror on his face makes me realize the stench and scene are as bad as I think.

Bill holds out a plastic bag and says, "The nurse said you may need this."

I reach inside and pull out a disposable diaper. The words and actions of the driver, police officer, and nurse suddenly make sense: they recognized my predicament before I did.

"No," I said. "I'm not wearing this."

Further in the bag is a long pair of disposable pants that look like hospital scrubs. "Ok, I can handle this," I say happily.

Bill says, "What, with nothing underneath?"

"Yes," I tell him. "You can't see through them. Besides, we're going home from here."

Bill nods, not about to argue.

"Ah," I smile, reaching into the bag. "A package of soapy wet wipes! Now, that's what I'm talking about!"

I start cleaning myself, the floor, the sink, the faucets. I think I'm doing a good job when Bill points to the back of my left leg.

I ask, "What?"

Bill takes a few wipes and begins to clean the back of my leg down to the mess that has pooled in my flip-flop. "Oh," I sigh. "Thanks."

I look at Bill and shake my head. "You know, if this situation was the other way around, I don't know if I'd be in here with you."

He smiles and gives me a look that says, "Yes, you would."

A born talker who never met a microphone she didn't like, Jackie Davis is a marketing maven and masterful storyteller. Endlessly creative yet admittedly lacking manual dexterity, she wields words as her artistic medium. Her Ivy League pedigree and 25+ HGTV appearances rarely get mentioned—she's too humble for that. You will find her an engaging speaker with a playful sense of humor who captivates audiences with wit and wisdom. Jackie is passionate about her volunteer activities which empower women and people of color. Though residing in Massachusetts, she and her husband still consider New York home. Visit linkedin.com/in/jackierdavis for more.

What is Love?

Four letters L-O-V-E, which carry so much hope and aspiration. But does LOVE live up to our expectations? Contemplating my experience, it doesn't fit the neat package I imagined. So, for good or bad, here is my messy love story.

WAR: Love is brave (or stupid.)

June 1992. I'm walking towards the exit of Budapest Airport wondering what the hell I am doing.

Someone had told me that there might be a bus going from Budapest in Hungary to Belgrade in Serbia.

In Europe, the Balkan Wars are into their second year and I haven't seen my Montenegrin boyfriend for a year. The authorities won't let him out and I can't fly in. Serbia and Montenegro have had sanctions placed against them by the International Community, including a ban on all flights. If I want to see him, I'm going to have to take some risks.

So, here I am taking my chances when fortune smiles upon me. As I walk out of the airport, I see a bus right in front of me with the destination clearly marked BELGRADE. I mentally pump my fist, marvelling at the unexpected ease of this first step. I get a ticket, much to the merriment of the driver and his friends who want to know what I'm doing travelling into a region that so many people are trying to escape from. The passengers on the bus are journalists and some locals returning to Serbia. Plus of course, one either very brave or stupid traveller, driven by love to reunite with her boyfriend.

Goran manages to get to Belgrade from the coast where he lives in Budva, ahead of me. Our reunion, if I describe it, is possibly worthy of a movie scene. But I won't. Against the backdrop of war and the horrors being perpetuated in its name, our romance pales into insignificance.

The prelude to this reunion was a five-year holiday romance. It had been fun, light-hearted and *absolutely NOT* serious. Neither of us had any desire for it to be more than what it was. Yet, when the war had started something changed.

Perhaps it was the intensity of the conflict, or maybe the personal attacks and pain that Goran endured as a conscientious objector to the war. Our conversations turned deeper. It was a turning point for me. I realised

I was in trouble. I'd fallen. Hook. Line. Sinker. Right in the middle of a ferocious war.

The three days we spend together in Belgrade feel like a dream. We talk like we've never talked. We learn things about one another that we'd never shared before. Our curiosity runs deep. After five years of fun and light-hearted romance, there is so much we don't know about each other and we are both eager to learn, explore and get to know and share the deepest parts of ourselves.

Three days of utter, naked vulnerability changes everything. And it seems it is not just me who has fallen in love.

PLANS: Love is hopelessly naïve.

January 1994. My strategy has failed.

After fifteen years living in the UK, I'm ready to go home, back to Australia. But there is an inconvenience complicating my return. Goran.

My heart knows how I feel, but my head doesn't want to accept it. I think my head needs to lead on this occasion. So, I concoct a plan. It's Winter, which I think will work in my favour.

All I need to do is spend three months in Budva with Goran and it will give me a taste of reality. That should be enough to shake off the romanticised veneer from this epic love drama. A drama that started as a holiday romance that went on for a few years. Light and heady times. Then the war. Dark and dramatic times fuelling passion and a deepening love.

See what I mean? It doesn't take a genius to recognise that these scenarios don't make for real life. Not in the longer term. How can a love like that endure in normal conditions?

So, my strategy was planned. The Balkan Wars were still raging, moving from Croatia to Bosnia and on to Kosovo. Sanctions had hit Montenegro hard and Winter was made even gloomier than usual because of electricity blackouts.

I quit my job and left London for Budva in November.

At first, the romance continued. Blackout nights were spent in our little apartment, snuggled in blankets, playing blackjack by candlelight, with pistachio nuts as our betting currency. Just the two of us.

Yet, as the weeks went on, Goran's drinking habit became apparent as he spent increasing time out with his friends. His father had died the year before and it had hit him hard, on top of the war, sanctions and a general feeling of hopelessness. We became fractious. Arguments followed. My strategy was playing out. Reality was revealing a future I did not want.

I tried to book an early flight back to London, but the only travel agent in town was run by a friend of

Goran's and I was told there were no flights. Exasperated, I knew his friend was lying. Those Budva boys had each other's backs, that's for sure. It didn't take long for Goran to get wind of my exit plans. He asked me to give us another chance.

Despite some reservations, I agreed.

To my surprise he got his act together and the weeks that followed drew us together, blowing apart my strategy.

So, here we now find ourselves in January 1994. I've told him I'm going back to Australia. I ask if he will come with me.

It's not as easy a question for him to answer as you may think. He loves his home. He loves his family— his Mum, Sister, Brother and Niece. He lived in LA in the US for awhile and saw that living in the West is not all it is trumped up to be. His land—the black mountains and Mediterranean Sea are a big part of him. The thought of leaving is hard.

However, I am resolute. I'm going home with or without him. I must do this. It's time.

At the last moment, the very last day before my flight to London, Goran makes his choice. He says yes. That last night we spend filling in the visa forms. We make our plans to meet in Athens in two months so we can fly to Australia together.

SEPARATION: Love is forgiving.

Sydney, September 2002. I've bought a house.

Did you notice the singular 'I'?

We are still 'we', kind of. And we are three. Our beautiful daughter Siena was born four years earlier. But I'm shielding myself with some independence.

The last few years have been hard. His drinking has taken a toll on our relationship. He tries to control it, setting rules like never drinking before sundown. He's never aggressive, but it is lonely living with an addict. We don't communicate well.

So, I called it quits on our relationship. After one too many battles, I finally accepted that the power alcohol had over him was greater than the power of love. He was heading to Montenegro to see his family and that was the moment I pulled the plug. We were renting our home at the time, but while he was away, I started looking for somewhere to buy for me and Siena.

After a couple of months, he started calling. At first, I didn't answer. When I eventually did, he said he loved us and didn't want to lose us. He told me he had quit drinking and whatever it took, he would do it for us as a family.

He sounded genuine, but I wasn't wholly convinced that he had the strength to keep it up. He'd tried before and failed. Yet, there was something in the way he said it this time that stopped me from closing the door on our relationship. I chose to keep it open, just a crack, along with my heart.

Still, I wasn't entirely prepared to commit moving forward as a 'we', so I went ahead and bought the house in my name.

He's back in our lives and we are taking one day at a time, in our new home together.

LIFE: Love is messy.

Sydney, May 2024. I'm writing this, contemplating whether to share our tumultuous love story.

Are you wondering whether he was true to his word about quitting drinking?

He was.

He quit.

To this day I'm in awe of how he did it. No help, no support group. He just made his decision and stuck to it.

In the meantime, life happened. Good times and challenging ones, like everyone else. The ups and downs less intense than when we were younger, but we still have them.

Years ago, I remember watching a documentary where an older couple spoke about their relationship through warm loving smiles, saying "we always knew we'd be together forever."

I can't relate to that.

Our love story is messy; our characters flawed. There has never been or ever will be certainty of outcome. What we have is a recognition that we've both been in the arena and given it our all. We've done that because, whatever our story is and however it ends, it is and has been worth fighting for.

Based in Sydney, Australia, Carolyn Butler-Madden traded a successful marketing career for her 'second act' as a purpose activist. An award-winning business book author, speaker, podcast host, and consultant, Carolyn is on a mission to inspire businesses to lead with love for people and the planet. Beyond her activism, she enjoys travelling, good food, and spending time with family, friends, and Monty the Mini Groodle/Goldendoodle. Learn more at carolynbutlermadden.com

Upstairs Love

We forget to remember that
Love only exists in the "present time."
It may be "preserved" in art, writing or music,
To be reborn again in the present moment of another
time...

When Young Terry was nine years old, he began experiencing a recurring nightmare. These dreams coincided with a significant event in his life—watching the movie "Days of Wine and Roses" at a drive-in theater in Kingston, New York, with his parents and sister in the summer of 1963.

In this recurring dream, Young Terry finds himself trapped in the same static, prison-like scenario. He hovers just below the ceiling in a barely lit room, facing a two-walled corner and looking directly into the vertex where the walls and ceiling meet. Upon waking, he remembers the walls and ceiling as two shades of monochromatic gray with rough, textured surfaces. There was a muffled hum like the chirping of crickets that accompanied the dreams.

This nightmare occurred repeatedly between the ages of nine and ten years old. Young Terry didn't fully understand concepts like alcoholism at the time. Still, he could sense parallels between the movie's storyline and his family situation. The film had felt so real, the scenes so revealing, it may have triggered his unsettling dreams.

Ralph Sr. and Rachel's home.

Young Terry and his little sister Susan grew up in the home of their grandparents Ralph Sr. and Rachel, where they had moved after their father Richard Jr. came back from the second world war. Ralph Sr. had passed away and upon Ralph Jr.'s return, Rachel moved into the upstairs suite.

The home was a rectangular, yellow brick house located in Saugerties, New York. The exterior of the home featured carefully curated landscapes. Two tall pine trees arched over the front walkway while Japanese Barberry bushes grew beneath the French windows. The property boasted extensive gardens,

showcasing the couple's passion for cultivation.
Flower beds lined each side of the house, with a long
bed of white Lily of the Valley along the driveway
The backyard was a testament to thoughtful design
and horticultural knowledge. It featured a brick-
walled terrace, various trees including yew and white
birch, beds of mixed tulips, and a meandering bed of
ivy enclosed by stacked bluestones. A centerpiece of
the backyard was an elaborate water feature—a koi
pond fed by an artificial stream that transited
through five smaller pools.

Inside, the house exuded an air of refined taste and
intellectual pursuit. The living room and dining area
had ten-foot ceilings adorned with five floor-to-
ceiling French windows and two French doors. The
furniture reflected mid-century modern aesthetics,
with oak lounge chairs and a matching loveseat.
Bookshelves lined the walls, filled with classic
studies, history, and literature, as well as picture
books of world-famous paintings and digests of
flowers and birds.

This environment, curated with great affection by
Ralph Sr. and Rachel, was one of beauty, elegance,
and respectability. It represented a way of "being"
and "seeing" the world distinct from Young Terry's
parents' outlook and it made the children yearn for

what they felt and saw in their grandparents' way of
life.

This persistent yearning—coupled with the hunger to
eat breakfast on Saturday mornings, which the
parents would not wake up to prepare (nor had left
the kitchen stocked so the six- and ten-year-olds
could help themselves)—led the children upstairs to
seek out their grandmother, Rachel.

Miraculously, the chaos and dysfunction of life with
their parents at the lower level of their home didn't
follow Young Terry and Susan as they made their
escape to the enlightened and gracious presence of
their grandmother on the second floor.

Rachel's kitchen.

Rachel's kitchen was modest in size but featured a four-burner gas stove where their grandmother would cook for her grandchildren. The kitchen table, covered with a distinctive red oilcloth, had a warm and inviting atmosphere where the ravenous Young Terry and Susan would sit while Rachel prepared their meals.

The menu typically included:

1. Eggs—either fried or scrambled, according to the children's preference.

2. Fried bologna —a simple but satisfying addition to the breakfast.

3. Toast—served with buckwheat honey, adding a touch of sweetness to the meal.

This breakfast was again, in stark contrast to what the children might find downstairs in their parents' kitchen, where they often had to make do with cereal (if there was milk available) or chunks of Velveeta cheese.

Rachel's cooking and the warmth of her kitchen provided both physical and emotional sustenance. The act of preparing and sharing these simple but lovingly made meals became a significant part of

Young Terry and Susan's positive memories of the grandmother and their time in the upstairs portion of the house.

After breakfast, Rachel and the children would often move into her bedroom to watch Saturday morning cartoons on her small black and white TV, extending the comforting routine beyond the meal.

The nightmare ends.

The nightmares continued until a pivotal moment on February 9, 1964. On this date, Young Terry watched The Beatles' first appearance on The Ed Sullivan

Show with his grandmother Rachel. The joy and hope they experienced together while watching The Beatles perform profoundly affected him. He saw them playing sophisticated songs with genuine passion, which offered him a message of hope he could dream about.

This hope was amplified by the woman sharing this moment with him. The one who had shown him that love can shine through even the darkest of times. The recurring nightmare stopped.

Young Terry isn't entirely sure how that happened. Maybe it was the pure delight of watching The Beatles that provided a counterbalance to the anxieties represented in his nightmares.

Maybe it was just time for him to move past this troubling period in his young life—and remember that there was love. And hope.

He now had a much better dream.

Art is an entity of love,
Preserved in a past moment of presence,
So a present moment of love may arrive,
At a future moment in time.

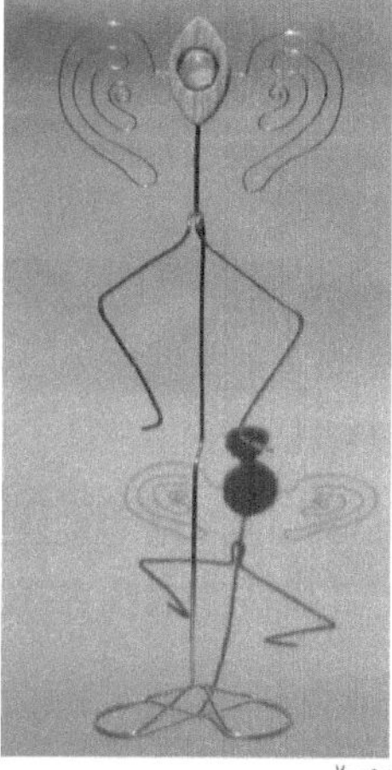

"Good Listener, Open Mind"

Terry Hayes, media professional turned visual artist, brings a wealth of experience to his creative pursuits. With roots in the Hudson Valley and four years of Navy service, Terry's journey into media production included high-profile projects like Madonna's Vogue video and NFL commercials. A cum laude graduate in Media and Communications, he now channels his expertise into sculpting, guitar playing and writing. Terry's unique "sticky geometry" artwork merges metaphysics with organic mathematics. Currently, he's passionate about promoting Japanese craftsmanship culture and developing intentional community portals, aiming to revitalize American artistry and workmanship. Terry's career evolution embodies his commitment to creativity and cultural exchange.

"This fire that we call Loving is too strong for human minds. But just right for human souls."

-Aberjani

PART 3

Love is:

a revelation.

Like Father, Like Son

Whenever I pick up a hammer or screwdriver and wander around the house, I can feel my wife's eyes lock onto me like laser beams, tracking my every move. Even if she doesn't say it out loud, I hear the words "Don't Norm-ify it!" echoing around inside my cavernous skull. Those words are always in the stern voice of my lovely, long-suffering spouse, Lady Pamela[3].

It's happening again this morning as I gather tools and devise a plan to deal with the mud in our family room problem. Our exuberant Yellow Labrador, Mickey, regularly paints our family room floor with

---

[3] Her royalty-loving family bestowed this honorific title on her as a child. I continue to use it to esteem her lightheartedly.

muddy footprints whenever he comes in from the backyard. I'm dubbing this operation "Project Mud-Free Mickey".

Lady Pamela senses I've moved into 'Project Mode' and warns me, "Whatever you're up to, Buster, don't Norm-ify it!". I hear it in a tone of voice that tells me she means business. She believes she has ample reason to be wary of my prowess as a handyman.

The "Norm" she is referring to is my father, Norman Arthur Drouillard. He was the man for whom the phrase, "Jack of all trades, master of none" was created. He was bold and brave enough to attempt many things in life, but sadly, most of his handyman efforts yielded decidedly unmasterful results.

I've always aspired to achieve breathtaking levels of craftsmanship in all that I do, but with the dad I had and the training I received from him, it's been awfully hard to reprogram my genes or denature my nurture.

As a child of want who grew up during the Great Depression, my father was pained to throw anything out. Whenever he came across a short length of wood, a rusty piece of metal, or a scrap of wire, he'd say, "it might come in handy someday." So, we kept it. We had impressive junk piles of wood scraps, angle iron, copper pipes, plus buckets of bent nails and screws, and half-empty cans of paint. It was our own little Home Depot, conveniently located right behind the work shed.

His propensity to re-use or re-purpose whatever materials we had on hand generated a 'reverse Midas touch' around our home. Something golden would often be transformed into something less alluring. For example, a broken handle on a kitchen drawer could be replaced with the driver's door handle from a '55 Ford Fairlane. "There. Another project done", he'd say with satisfaction.

Thriftiness gave our 4-acre hobby farm a distinctive, "Who would have done it that way?" kind of look. For instance, the wooden fence around our pasture was always 'mud-colored'. Every few years, we'd re-paint it using whatever bits of paint we had lying around. All the leftover cans of paint, no matter what color or composition—interior or exterior, water or oil-based—they'd all get dumped into a 5-gallon pail. Astonishingly, the resulting color was invariably the same - mud. I suspect 'mud' may be a color more dominant than any of the three so-called primary colors.

To save money when our farmhouse was constructed, we had some rooms left unfinished. It was up to my dad to finish the plumbing, electrical, and drywall installation. These rooms included my parents' ensuite bathroom and a main floor powder room under the stairs. My dad had to install long runs of copper pipe from the utility room to the unfinished bathrooms. In both cases, amidst all the elbows and other fittings he had to solder into the pipelines, he lost track of which pipe would carry the cold versus the hot water. And he wouldn't know which was which until he turned the water on.

As his luck would have it, both sinks ended up with the hot and cold taps reversed. It was really not a problem for our family. We quickly learned "the cold is on the left and the hot is on the right" and we got used to it, but it was often entertaining to hear the shrieks whenever a guest used the powder room. I'll admit though, it was always a little off-putting having the toilet fill up with hot water. It was our own hillbilly bidet, I guess.

Perhaps it did not inspire Lady Pamela's confidence in me when I told her that some of my dad's projects were downright dangerous. Like the time I came home from university for the Christmas holidays and couldn't believe what was about to happen.

We were preparing to host our annual extended family gathering. Over 50 relatives were soon to arrive, and he excitedly pulled me over to show me a

contraption he had built in the back of our open gas
fireplace. It was a small industrial fan he had
mounted just above the flames. The purpose was to
prevent all that "wasted heat", as he put it, from
going up the chimney. Instead, the fan would blow
the hot exhaust air into the family room.

"Imagine how much faster this room will heat up!"
he said proudly.

"Imagine how much faster we're all going to die!" I
said loudly as I yanked that menacing contraption out
of the fireplace alcove. "Dad, there's a good reason
fireplaces have chimneys. We don't live in a cave."

You had to give him full marks for trying to do his
best, at least.

Having an in-house handyman was to my great
benefit. From a toddler's age, I was my father's
apprentice. I got years of training and learned to
mimic his indispensable handyman habits.

As a kid, I sometimes resented spending every
Saturday following my father around doing repairs
around our home or at the rental houses he fixed up
and sold. But in my teens, I considered these skills to
be a great asset that I would bring into my future
marriage. "Oh," I'd tell myself, "What a lucky girl

she'll be!"

However, during the years of our courtship and early marriage, Lady Pamela came to see things differently. It didn't take her long to size up what she had gotten herself mixed up with.

Sure, I heard her many suggestions like, "This leak doesn't seem to be slowing down. Should we call a plumber?" and "Those sparks scare me. Shouldn't we contact an electrician for this?" But I always brushed aside her concerns with a confident, "No need to call anyone. I saw how my dad fixed this once."

Her wariness regarding my handyman skills has never abated. If anything, she remains on high alert.

This morning as I start the Mud-Free Mickey project, I take a pencil and sit down to sketch a plan on the back of an envelope. This is something I'd rarely seen my father do. On most occasions, he figured out how to do something long after the project was underway.

I'm thinking that coming up with a plan beforehand will surely protect me from Norm-ifying this project.

Nevertheless, I vow to faithfully follow my dad's tried-and-true approach to construction. I will (1) keep the design as simple as possible and (2) use only whatever materials I have lying around.

I recall we have some random-sized scraps of plywood leftover from a previous not-so-successful project. Immediately, a brilliant idea illuminates the interior of my skull. Even my eye sockets light up.

My plan is to simply lay the random-sized pieces of plywood on the ground outside the patio doors. I'll let the plywood follow the natural downward slope of the land because that will allow the rain to wash off the mud as needed. Presto! This design comes with a built-in auto-cleaning feature. I consider the plan to be a stroke of genius in both its simplicity and utility.

With a swelling chest, I present the design to my wife and expect effusive accolades to soon smother me. But that's not how things are rolling out.

Immediately, her countenance changes into a contortion almost not humanly possible.

A minute passes. Her face emerges from its near catatonic state, and she announces, "Your father would be proud of you."

I know that to be the Kiss of Death.

"Gimme that pencil," she demands. "How about sinking some short 4x4 posts here, here, here, and here? Join them with some supporting beams and then lay some 1x4s across for a deck. Do you think you can do that? And keep it level, for Pete's sake! 'Follow the natural downward slope of the land?' What junkyard were you raised in?"

I magnanimously choose to use her design and abandon my own. Outside we go.

Several hours later, with her constant coaching and correction, I manage to get the deck built to her specifications and satisfaction. It looks great and I'm sure it will serve us well for many years.

Later that afternoon, as I'm sitting on a camp chair on this new and level deck, I bask in the sunshine, quaff a brew or two, and ruminate. Sometimes, I tell myself, it just takes a little more time for someone to recognize the giftedness in the other. That's not a problem. I can wait.

Gary Drouillard is a minor-league award-winning short story writer and essayist, known for his nutbar sense of humor, his piercing portrayals of what matters most in life, and for having an overly inflated view of himself. He is currently nestled in Windsor, Ontario, luxuriating in a post-career afterlife, dabbling in hobbies like reading, writing, and bike riding. Those are all activities for which he had little time when he was busy pioneering the expansion of international roaming for Canadian wireless customers. That initiative satisfied the desire of his own heart, to make it easy for everyone to GO AWAY.

Autumn Leaves

It's a chilly autumn afternoon when I set out with my kids on the number 72 bus—the scenic route along the Seine into central Paris.

We get off at Trocadéro, with its unbroken view of the Eiffel Tower just across the river.

We've trodden this path before. My children know exactly where we're going, and they are very excited.

First, a ride for my son on the old-fashioned merry-go-round on the Right Bank of the Seine. I stand and watch, waving as he comes into view each time astride his white horse, the familiar smell of hot sugared peanuts from the vendor nearby wafting towards us. Then we cross over the bridge to stand in the massive presence of the Eiffel Tower.

My three-year-old is in awe of this construction, and
he can't believe this is the venue for our school-
holiday, autumn leaf-crunching expedition.

In the Champ de Mars park in front of the tower lie
piles and piles of crispy brown and orange and yellow
leaves, ripe for stomping and jumping and falling in.

I release my just-walking daughter from her
pushchair, and like a little wind-up toy she toddles
off towards them, her pointy pink hood bobbing as
she goes.

My son drops to his knees in an especially thick pile,
scooping up armfuls, throwing them in the air like
confetti, and whooping with joy.

I keep an eye on my little daughter, who is wont to set
off on her own explorations. But mostly we play
together in the mass of autumn crunchiness. The
sounds and scents of the city are replaced in those
moments by a very real connection with the cycles of
nature.

We round off the expedition with an ice-cream. My
son takes a few licks of his cone, then, very sweetly,
holds it out to my daughter—not yet of ice-cream
cone age—so that she can taste. She's now safely back
in her pushchair, and kicks her little legs with glee.
Getting to share something with her big brother is a
big deal.

That autumnal afternoon was replete with meaning,
for it marked the end of an era.

Paris was the city I had escaped to when I couldn't
find my place in the vastness of London. It was where
I had begun my career proper, met my husband, and
where my children were born. Over the years there I
had lived in eight different flats, my favourite being
the little garret studio in a 19th-century building
overlooking Père Lachaise cemetery.

But for all its beauty, it had become an unwieldy big
city for me with small children in tow. In just a few
weeks' time we would move to Barcelona. There I'd be
starting again in a country where, this time, I didn't
speak the language. And where we were to live outside
the city, by the sea. Like all changes in my life, I was
greeting our forthcoming move with a mix of nervous
excitement and trepidation.

This excursion was my opportunity to enjoy Paris at
its most emblematic, and in my favourite season too.
A chance to say goodbye.

It remains one of my most poignant memories of a
city I had loved, and of who I had become in my time
in France. Of my two cherished little ones, and of
young motherhood, which I had embraced with every
piece of my heart and soul.

Caroline Harvey is a public speaking coach and trainer who grew up in Wales, the 'Land of Song'. She has lived and worked in several countries across Europe, and in Japan. When not pulling together threads, and weaving them into stories, Caroline is on a mission to help people cut through the noise without shouting—leveraging their voice and natural presence to confidently drive change. She lives south of Barcelona, where the mountains meet the sea. Her two children having flown the nest, she lives with a curly-haired brown dog called Phoebe. Visit carolineharvey.me for more.

What is Love?

'**M**ummy, what is love?' I hear you ask. You are four years old, and your small hand is in mine.

Your arm reaches up trustingly, the way it always does, for that familiar grasp.

You could already hold on fiercely when you were only a few hours old. Your tiny fist clenched tight around my pinky finger. I felt my heart expand in my chest as your gaze met mine, as if it was being filled with a thousand balloons all bursting at once with the breathless wonder of it all.

I knew then that I would never know love quite like this ever again.

Except I was wrong.

It happened over and over and over again as I watched
you learn to first roll and then crawl onto all fours.

Then one day with that look of determination and like
the notion had never before occurred to you that you
could, you took your first teetering step. And then
another and then a third until you fell back down on
your bottom clapping your hands together
delightedly with the joy of it.

I felt that swell of pride rise once more in my chest
like a huge wave knocking me off my feet.

'You're so clever! I beamed besottedly, smothering
you in a hug as if you had just flown to the moon and
back or solved world peace.

It wouldn't be the last time I was moved to tears at
the magnitude of the smallest of moments.

Quite the contrary, this was one of so many moments
we would share as you first spoke my name or pointed
earnestly at the night sky and said the single word,
'MOON!'

So, this is love.

I hear it when I ask before you go to sleep at night,
'Do you want to know a secret?'

And you always say yes as you snuggle down in your
bed, even though I've told you so many times that it's
no longer a secret.

'I love you so much' I whisper and the truth of it
stings my eyes. Every. Single. Time.

I smell it when you wrap your arms around me and
my nose nuzzles into your neck. Unforgettably,
adorably, you.

I taste it when I'm feeding you and you take the spoon
in your hand and put it to my mouth, the sweetness of
porridge and the look of sheer delight that you are
now feeding me.

Was that the first time I noticed that look of glee—all
cheekiness and bright-eyed laughter—that will
become your signature and have us all in raptures so
much of the time?

So, love. I can feel it. Right here, right now swelling in
my chest again as you ask the question.

But I don't know how to describe it.

I know that love is all around us.

I can see it and feel it all the time if I take the time to look carefully and notice.

I know it's like a huge magnet that draws people and things and places towards me.

An invisible, gravitational pull.

I know that love is a compass guiding you to your true north.

It's a cape that I will wrap around you to keep you safe.

And I know that if I ever lost you, I couldn't bear the unimaginable pain of it.

I want to say all of this and more as I try to answer this simplest of questions.

But I don't.

Instead, I look down at you and smile.

'Love is you and me' I say as we walk hand-in-hand. I love you and you love me and that's all that matters.

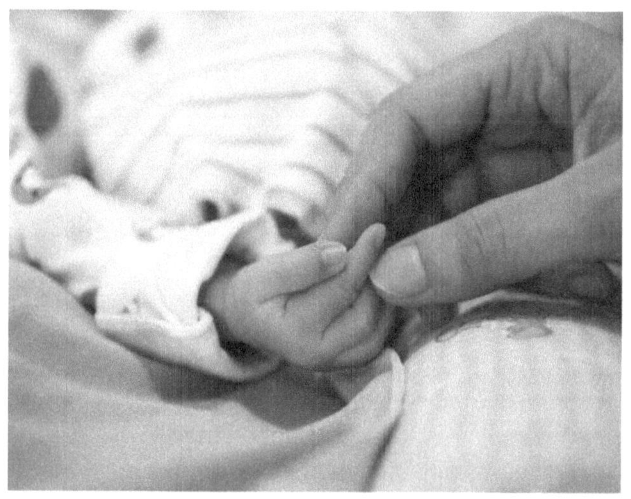

Cat Preston has always been happiest when she's able to connect and share stories over a nice cup of tea. Whether she's coaching creatives to unleash their unique gifts or sharing the stories of everyday heroes and change-makers on her podcast, 'Collective Wisdom,' she understands everyone has a story worth telling—and listening to. Life has taken her across the globe, and seeing the world through that multicultural lens has taught her to question narratives and embrace curiosity. Discover more about what inspires Cat and how she helps unlock the real-life magic within at catpreston.com

Does He Love Me?

For two years, I hadn't been able to look at other people's children without crying. Now, I was holding one in my arms. It wasn't mine. I was sitting on the sofa at a friend's place, cradling her first baby. How precious, how fragile this little bundle was.

I glanced at my ex-boyfriend, sitting on a chair opposite me.

Seven years of love and companionship, adventures and challenges. We thought we could overcome anything together. Until one morning, two years earlier when I found out I was pregnant. I knew that he never wanted to have children. Afraid of losing him, we went to a clinic to end the pregnancy and never spoke about it again.

But after this, I knew in my bones: I wanted to have a child. With all my heart and soul. I mentioned this to my boyfriend casually from time to time—don't scare him—and he said, yes, one day, maybe . . . I clung to that. One day.

Life went on until we learned that good friends of ours had split up after many years together. She had always wanted children; he didn't. She loved him and accepted his choice, until he suddenly left her for someone else, and her child-bearing age was over.

I wondered, would I face the same situation one day? Would I hold my boyfriend "hostage" because I had given up my dream of having a child, for him? A few days later, I decided to have "that talk" with him over dinner at a restaurant. I needed to know: would he be ready to have a child with me? Now, not "one day." Did he love me enough to say yes?

I went right to the heart of the matter: "I really need, I really want to have a child with you. Are you in it with me?" After a brief pause, he responded.

"If you really want to have a child, you have to do it with someone else."

I felt time grind to a halt. Total silence. At that moment, we both knew our relationship was over. I left the restaurant, tears streaming down my face. I felt so unloved, so hurt, so rejected. All I could think was, he doesn't love me. How else could he push me away like this?

Sitting on the sofa now, with my friend's baby in my arms, I thought back to that conversation and felt a mix of awkward emotions. My ex-boyfriend was looking at me, and I imagined him thinking how ridiculous I looked with this baby in my arms.

While I waited for him to make some kind of joke, he suddenly smiled and said quietly, "You're going to be a great mom one day."

Something opened up inside me at that moment, though I didn't know what it was. Now, looking back 23 years later, I realize that by saying no to having a child together, he had been brave enough to tell me his truth. This WAS love—tough love—and it had set me free.

Raised in former East Germany, Andrea Bernard's world expanded after the fall of the Berlin Wall. She seized opportunities to travel, living in Japan and France while mastering English, French, and Japanese alongside her native German. After a rich career as a multilingual writer, journalist, and translator, she is today pivoting to nursing to pursue her passion for caring for others. Andrea lives near Paris with her husband, son, and two rambunctious German Rex cats. A practicing Buddhist, she finds solace in meditation and loves sharing stories that inspire love and compassion.

The Year I Fell in Love
with Flowers

I look up *flower* in my thesaurus

and find *angiosperm*:

"Flowering plants that produce

seeds in an ovary"

perhaps that's it,

the connection, the wound

the garden heals—

the need to mother.

The pansy has always been

a favourite for its boldness,

it's whimsy, but this year

a disappointment:

late, pithy blossoms

a let-down when things

don't work out as you'd hoped

but still, vestiges of joy,

all the other progeny

showing up anyway.

I feel an affinity with

the steady, reliable impatiens,

also those snap dragons

grandmother's favourite

teasing with their surprising

bountiful late blooms

she would tell us

to squeeze the flower

to open its mouth—

"That's why it's called

a snapdragon!"

The marigolds also had

a second performance

but can finally rest

natural defenders against

the garden's common pests,

nasturtium too, sprout fresh buds

deep in the season

offering seeds for next year

how could I not adore

these industrious providers,

good company for the

garden's elders, the geraniums,

welcoming hosts

to all the newcomers.

We pay homage to all of this

like returning family

who come as they will:

some early, some late,

some predictably unpredictable,

showing up when they choose

with nothing other than themselves,

but we welcome them

with love anyway

just as they are,

however they arrive.

Leanne Fournier writes fiction, nonfiction, and poetry in the stunning wilderness of Northwestern Ontario, Canada. Her creative work is infused with vivid imagery and a profound sense of place, evident in her beautifully illustrated poetry collection. The collection explores the contradictions and parallels she sees around human connection and belonging—and is set to be released in 2025. Leanne founded MightyWrite—Write for Business, where she helps clients tell stories with clarity and impact and find their unique voice. A passionate writer and social justice advocate, Leanne publishes stories about the people most often unseen and unheard at mightywrite.substack.com.

Baby Beach

The sand is warm. Lying on our backs, holding hands, breathing deeply. The sky is pitch black, dotted with starlight.

The small waves are loud. Repeating ssshhhhhhh, ssshhhhhh, ssshhhhhh.

The water is darker than the sky. Darker than molasses. Darker than the darkest earth.

Light from a trillion stars shimmers on the water.

I love the sky. I love the stars.

I love you.

A trance of time passes.

We get up. Walk slowly. Hand in hand.

A single streetlight illuminates the trail to the top of
the bluff.

I turn back to the water. The white crests of the waves
gently meet the shore.

The blackness.

The stars. You.

I am not dreaming this dream.

*As someone who is often moved to tears by the artistry
that animates music, cooking, and photography, Dave
Lewis writes stories that invoke an appreciation for
beauty and celebrate an earnest pursuit of love. These are
stories that his readers find to be moving, too. He resides
in Minneapolis, Minnesota, with his wife Jan Elftmann.*

Off Leash

I'm riding my bicycle on an asphalt path along the Charles River in Boston. It's a beautiful spring day. The sun is shining, not a cloud in the sky. I'm using the bicycle path so I can enjoy the ride and not have to worry about maneuvering around parked cars and traffic.

I don't have a specific route in mind. I'm not trying to beat my best time or to go further than my previous ride. This ride is purely to enjoy being outdoors and exercising.

I'm wearing a bright orange and red bicycle jersey. The kind of colors that are so bright that your eyes feel like they're burning if you stare at the jersey for too long. I'm also wearing cycling shorts. My legs look like chicken legs sticking out of the black spandex shorts. If you look at me from the back, the padding looks like I stuffed some biscuits into my shorts to use as cushioning. No one looks good in bicycle attire.

Ahead I see an adult walking and a silhouette off to the side. The unidentified figure has short, cropped hair. I keep riding, approaching the person and the outline of the other. What I'm closing in on begins to come into focus.

It's a person with a dog off the leash. The dog is sniffing the ground as if he's in search of a T-bone steak.

I love all animals. But dogs can be so unpredictable around me. I never know how they're going to react towards me, so I worry. I worry that they will hurt me.

One morning years ago, I encountered my neighbor, Bob. Bob's companion was a beautiful shaggy dog like you see in the old Disney movies. The dog's name was Frizz. He had so much fur I was unable to see his eyes or mouth. So, I asked Bob if it would be okay for me to pet Frizz. He told me that Frizz is friendly.

I naturally moved my hand towards Frizz.

He started to bark and growl at me.

I jerked my hand away from Frizz. I felt my pulse quicken. I walked away with a friendly wave to Bob. Bob said loudly that Frizz had never done that before. But I'm not so sure.

Another unexpected meeting was with one of those cute small dogs that people take with them everywhere. One of those dogs, Sprout, lived in the house where I rented an apartment.

I was preparing to leave for work. Locking my front door. My back was toward the door that led to the other part of the house.

Without warning, I felt Sprout biting my pant leg and realized that Sprout ran out from the door behind me. I felt his small teeth scratching my skin. I shook my leg back and forth to get Sprout to release my slacks. My trouser leg was shredded by this cute little dog.

The owner was horrified. Grabbed the dog in his arms and apologized. Offered to pay for a new pair of slacks.

I didn't even make eye contact with Sprout, but he still tried to use me as his own personal chew toy.

On another occasion, I was helping a friend deliver newspapers. I ran toward the front door to avoid getting wet by the lawn sprinklers.

Out of nowhere I saw a Doberman Pinscher racing at me.

Before I could react, the dog latched onto my right arm. The way the dog chomped on my arm you would think he was eagerly biting into a piece of raw meat. Not a person's arm.

I screamed. I started to cry. Through my tears I could see blood running down my arm onto the grass. Like gravy from roast beef prepared rare.

The owners were in the driveway washing their car.

When they heard my scream. They came running. And called the dog off.

I continued sobbing as they patched me up. I still have the scars.

When I see the dog off the leash along the Charles
River bike path my radar goes up. Even if he appears
to be innocently smelling what's around.

I'm concerned how the dog will react to me when I
ride past him. I consider slowing down and staying far
behind but I'm riding my bike for exercise, and I
would be riding too slowly to get a good workout.

I could turn around and go back from where I started
but there's no guarantee that I wouldn't come upon
another dog off the leash.

I decide to glide far to my left to pass. After passing
the dog and owner in tow I start to cruise toward the
right side of the path.

My front tire snags an indentation in the asphalt. I'm
set off balance. My arm is flung into the air. I'm no
longer seated. Slightly airborne. Gravity takes hold.
My helmet, protecting my head, crashes to the
pavement.

Cracking.

My feet are still attached to the bike via toe straps.

I'm lying on the path.

Slowly maneuvering to get myself to a seated
position.

I feel like I've been beaten up. I have a painful case of road rash, ripped bike shorts and an arm that has lost its strength. My arm feels rubbery.

The dog and owner catch up to me. My body is shaking. My breath is shallow and rapid.

Because I'm sitting on the ground my face is at the same height at the dog's mouth.

The dog approaches me. I can feel my heart thumping in my chest. I'm unable to stand up. I'm defenseless.

I sit as still as I can. Trying to slow down my breathing. I'm attempting to imitate a statue. We're face to face. The dog's sniffing my face. I can feel his moist nose brush against my face as he's assessing me.

I guess I pass the dog's test because the dog starts to lick my face. But this enrages me.

I'm livid. This whole event happened because I was trying to avoid the dog. "Leash your dog," I yell at the top of my lungs.

The human shrugs, then they and their dog turn silently and walk away together. I sit there cradling my limp arm and watch them go.

I sigh.

For the first time since I saw the dog off the leash, I'm calm. I'm relieved.

I find comfort in the fact that the dog showed me compassion. That the dog tried to show me some affection. An indication that, its owner's indiscretion aside, I was safe to be near him.

Maybe this will help me when I encounter other dogs. Thinking of him may help me to stop worrying so much. And once the worry subsides, I'll be able to open my heart.

Susan E. draws cartoons and tells stories for enjoyment and to entertain friends and family. She's constantly on the lookout for moments she wants to use to craft stories and illustrations. For Susan, moments are as ubiquitous as gulls snatching sandwiches at the seashore. But if she doesn't scribble these moments on scrap paper when she notices them, they may fly away. Susan's stories and drawings frequently feature animals, plants, and creatures. Her pursuits also include hiking, open water swimming, half marathons, and consuming massive quantities of chocolate.

The Gift of Trust

For years, my Dad struggled with drug addiction. But since we lived in different towns, it wasn't always top of mind for me. It had been years since I'd heard from him. Then out of nowhere, he called me saying that he wanted to come and visit me at my home.

My brother was against it. "Don't let him come over!" he said with a scowl. "And don't give him ANYTHING he could sell for drugs."

He thought I was naive, but I didn't care. I told my dad to come over and I would welcome him with open arms.

The day he was to arrive, I waited on the couch anxiously. Then I heard the knock.

"Aaaah, hi Daddy!" I say with excitement.

I reach out and give him a hug. As I squeeze him, I can

feel his bones. He feels skinny and frail. I loosen up my grip. I can tell he's not doing well. I look him in the eyes. He's not high, but he's not well.

I invite him to come in. We sit and talk, and laugh, and reminisce. We go in and out of topics like we're trying to make up for lost years within this one small moment. We talk long and fast as if neither of us knows when we'll see each other again.

Somehow the topic turns to technology and computers. Since he's been out, he feels he's out of step. He doesn't have a smartphone or computer. I tell him to hold tight and without a second thought, I go to my bedroom and grab my old laptop. It's still in perfect working condition. "Here, have this."

He says no, but I'm persistent.

He starts to cry.

But our time has come to an end.

So, we wipe our tears and say our goodbyes.

My heart is full of hope.

Over and done (the prayer).

A few years go by, and my dad continues to struggle. He goes back and forth, up and down while my heart goes from hope to hurt, hope to hurt.

It feels like I'm on a never-ending roller coaster of emotions. I can't quite find my footing.

I care for my dad, but I need to let him go. I can't keep cultivating hope and engaging in proactive interventions that wear me out and leave me depleted. I need to live my life and give him up to the divine. I finally find peace when I decidedly give him up and let go of hope.

For years, this works. Out of sight, out of mind. It's been about five years since I moved further south and I haven't seen, talked to, or had any interactions with my dad. I don't even think about him anymore.

But one weekend when I was at church, a guest pastor came for a special service to raise money for a non-profit project. He's doing his talk then towards the end he asked the congregation to give and think of one person we want to extend a prayer of salvation for.

He goes on to say not to just think of anyone, but to actually pray and ask God who we should believe for.

I closed my eyes and tried to think of a person I would like to see changed.

But my mind is blank.

I keep my eyes closed and try to search for a name.

Still nothing.

Finally, I ask quietly, "Who should I believe for?"

Out of nowhere, my dad comes to mind.

"Oh no, not this again!"

I start to argue with God. I'm not going there. My hope has expired. I don't want to start trying to believe again, just to get hurt.

The more I argue, the stronger the urge to write my dad's name down gets.

Fine!!!

I write down, Daddy, and put the paper and financial gift inside the basket near the front altar of the church. I feel butterflies and a flutter of nervousness. but I am not sure if that's a good sign or bad.

Nothing happens for months. Then, out of the blue, my brother tells me that my dad is in Oakland, in Northern California, and has been clean for almost a year. I'm shocked but in the back of my mind, I thought it probably wouldn't last.

A gift returned.

Fast forward a few years later and I hear my dad is married and is still clean.

Wow, now I'm in amazement. I can't help but think back to that night many moons ago when I added his name to the basket.

The next time I visit my hometown, in Northern California, I go to see him.

As we talk, I notice he sounds and looks good. He's even gained quite a few marriage pounds around his waist. Within every other sentence, I see glimpses of his old whimsical self; just a little more tattered and worn.

When I ask him what it feels like to be clean and how he managed to come out of it, he says hold on a minute. Then goes to his bedroom, digs around at the top of his closet, and pulls out this thick clunky-looking laptop.

"Look at this. Do you remember this?"
I'm like no . . .

"It looks like a very old computer," I say with a chuckle.

"Does it still work?"

 "Yes, yes!—but look at it!"

Ok??? It's an HP and??

Just then, he cuts me off and says:

"This is the computer that you gave me when I visited you at your house all those years ago. I kept it! It reminds me of who I am, and the love you, my daughter, have for me."

I am flabbergasted. We are both filled with emotion. I can't believe he held on to this old brick of a computer for all these years. My heart melts like butter as I think about what it must have meant for him to carry this thing for ten plus years.

The gift I gave is now the gift I receive as my dad is now clean and sober and is in great spirits.

Enrika Greathouse is a creative entrepreneur and community builder. As the founder of Small Gorilla Marketing, she crafts innovative campaigns that blend art with storytelling. As the Community Advocate for the Story Republic, she champions connection through shared narratives. Through her workshops, writing, and speaking engagements, Enrika explores how play, creativity, and human connection catalyze growth. No matter what she's up to, her passion lies in cultivating spaces where people can connect, create, and thrive together.

"When someone loves you, the way they say your name is different. You just know that your name is safe in their mouth."

-Billy, age 4

Afterword

From her kitchen window, my mother can see the two-up, two-down house where she was born. Looking up from the table, overlooking the garden, she faces the back bedroom window where my granny died. Mam can name every neighbour who has lived in any house on that road over the past eighty years. She has stories to ground her in this patch—the only place she feels she belongs.

My mam needed to stay close to those stories her entire life. I felt very differently. I wanted to leave and start a fresh chapter on my own blank page. I didn't understand when I left Dublin nearly forty years ago that I could never leave those stories behind. The lick of a 99 ice cream cone, a lungful of soda bread fresh from the oven, and the soft lilt of a shouted, 'howya' take me back.

There's an ancient Native American saying:

"Tell me the facts, and I'll learn. Tell me the truth, and I'll believe. But tell me a story, and it will live in my heart forever."

I know this to be true because I have seen it happen with my own eyes and felt it deep in my bones. Growing up in Dublin, the storytelling capital of the world, I saw first-hand how neighbours and friends created strong bonds from weak ties because of a shared story.

And through my work, helping people discover their storytelling skills, I've watched strangers become friends.

A few short months before the COVID-19 pandemic, we launched our first Story Skills Workshop. We had no idea how many people would sign up and were floored when 1,500 aspiring storytellers joined us. Since then, more than 5,000 people have taken the workshop, and some have joined our membership community, Story Republic.

I've witnessed people, most of whom have never met, become firm and loving friends by telling their stories. Some, like my mother, have stayed close to their origin stories; others, like me, have travelled afar. But we've all come to learn what we can't leave behind—and how sharing those stories carries us into a future, where, no matter how fragile our sense of belonging in our youth, we all belong.

We show up in community with open hearts to notice our lives, to practice, and to hear each other's stories. Those stories deserve to be shared with a wider audience and to spread far and wide. So, five years after our first workshop, we're launching Story Republic Press. The book you're holding and the stories within its pages were made possible by small acts of faith and love—which, at its heart, is storytelling. This anthology was made by a community of caring creators. It's a joy and a privilege to be part of their storytelling family. These everyday stories remind us to pay attention to

our lives and not simply let precious days slip by
unnoticed.

Proceeds

All proceeds from the 'What is Love?' are donated to support girls education via the non-profit CAMFED.

Learn more about this organization by visiting camfed.org

Acknowledgments

To Bernadette Jiwa for creating this community with
a loving, open heart.

And to Michael Averill for creating loving containers
within it.

Story Republic is a global community that encourages members to tell great stories from the heart. *What is Love?* is its first story collection. Learn more at storyrepublic.com

About the Editor

Rumi Tsuchihashi is an essayist who spreads the word about the life-changing joys of all things tiny. Her first book, *I Want To Remember This: Recognizing the Tiny Moments That Make Up a Life*, led to her 100-word essay, 'Where Our Palms Touch,' getting published the "Tiny Love Stories" column in the *New York Times*. As an editor and coach, Rumi helps emerging authors put potent stories and pocket-sized books out into world. Her upcoming book, *I Want This for Us: A Love Memoir in Miniature*, connects the dots of from heartbreak to second marriage in a series of vignettes.